A BRUTALLY HONEST GUIDE TO SUR-THRIVING GENERATION NOW

Your Personal Road Map to Planning for the Future While Living Today

GREGORY P. LAMONACA

A BRUTALLY HONEST GUIDE TO SUR-THRIVING GENERATION NOW YOUR PERSONAL ROAD MAP TO PLANNING FOR THE FUTURE WHILE LIVING TODAY

iUniverse books may be ordered through booksellers or by contacting:

iUniverse
1663 Liberty Drive
Bloomington, IN 47403
www.iuniverse.com
1-800-Authors (1-800-288-4677)

Because of the dynamic nature of the Internet, any web addresses or links contained in this book may have changed since publication and may no longer be valid. The views expressed in this work are solely those of the author and do not necessarily reflect the views of the publisher, and the publisher hereby disclaims any responsibility for them.

Any people depicted in stock imagery provided by Getty Images are models, and such images are being used for illustrative purposes only.
Certain stock imagery © Getty Images.

ISBN: 978-1-5320-6769-3 (sc)
ISBN: 978-1-5320-6768-6 (hc)
ISBN: 978-1-5320-6796-9 (e)

Library of Congress Control Number: 2019901522

Print information available on the last page.

iUniverse rev. date: 03/21/2019

Contents

A Letter from the Founder and Creator of Brutally Honest and LaMonaca Law

Welcome to LaMonaca Law and the Brutally Honest system. In this book and the LaMonaca Law site (www.LaMonacalaw.com) exist the passion, dedication, and heartfelt mission of LaMonaca Law and all my team members.

Brutally Honest was created by me and my friend (and former client) James Grim to address and confront the considerable difference between family law matters and all other areas of the law. In other areas of the law, individuals dispute an issue or an incident, appear in court, and never see each other again. In family law, however, matters involve spouses, children, parents, other family members, and friends, all of whom will most likely continue to be involved with one another for many years, if not for the rest of their lives.

Additionally, family law matters often include some of the most serious and emotional issues imaginable. At LaMonaca Law, our attorneys handle cases from the most basic to the extreme. Our team approach is designed to create a custom fit that matches a client's needs, wishes, budget, and goals to the individual attorney(s) and team members who can best address that client's unique situation. No two cases are the same, and because every case is different, each client needs to be handled differently based on his or her unique facts, circumstances, and goals.

For decades, the attorneys and other team members at LaMonaca Law have fought for the rights of our clients throughout the Main Line and beyond, practicing in the counties of Delaware, Chester, Montgomery, Philadelphia, Berks, and Lancaster and in concert with connections overseas in international matters as well.

At LaMonaca Law, we are proud assist clients with some of the extreme cases that other firms avoid, turn down, or refer to us. We have helped clients with any number of emotional, psychological, physical, or addictive conditions. Where other firms may shy away from such cases, LaMonaca Law embraces the needs of our clients and works diligently to assist them, starting with the initial meeting and continuing through the end of the case—and many times beyond. We recognize that whether a client's family law matters involves basic issues or the most complex problems, the client's emotional needs and underlying condition must be considered and addressed with care, compassion, and empathy. We have an extensive list of outside professionals to assist where needed, including counselors, psychologists, doctors, and many other experts to add to the client's team.

The Brutally Honest system addresses these unique aspects of family law cases and the emotions attendant to them. During the initial meeting with a client, I identify his or her fears, concerns, and goals. Through an array of techniques I have learned over decades of training, practice, and real-life implementation, I begin to change a client's state of mind from one of fear, concern, or any other negative to one of empowerment, focus, and clarity; I help clients see a compelling future for them and their families.

Through every successive meeting, clients encounter an approach that brings them high energy, focus, passion, and empathy that radically changes their emotions, attitudes, and beliefs. That process puts them at ease and reduces their fears, and they can redirect their energy and efforts toward the positive; they become empowered to pursue their and their families' best interests. Unlike other standard consultations, our Brutally Honest consultations helps our clients confront their emotions, fears, addictions, and conditions they may have bottled up for some time. I foster genuine trust, respect, and rapport with clients so they can feel comfortable and confident in opening up to me. Once they do, the results are transformative. While this realization presents itself in ways that are highly emotional for the clients, their courage to confront their very real emotions and concerns is the first step toward their creating compelling futures for themselves.

Over decades, the Brutally Honest system has evolved and now appears in books that describe the system and provide practical tools and techniques that allow people to replicate on their own much of what is done in my live, in-person meetings. Jim Grim and I wrote *The Brutally Honest Life Management Journal* for that purpose; it outlines the Brutally Honest process and allows readers to engage in self-guided journeys to reconnect with what matters most in their lives. Once they make that connection, they are equipped and empowered to move forward with their lives.

I followed the first book with *The Brutally Honest Pennsylvania Divorce & Custody Survival Guide* for my clients and potential clients; it's available on our website as a free download. Revisions to this book will be available in early 2019 with the new title being, "*The Brutally Honest Pennsylvania Divorce, Custody & Financial Survival Guide*. My purpose is to give you access to information and tools that you can immediately put to use even before we ever speak.

I wrote this book, the next iteration of the Brutally Honest brand, to give you the most up-to-date information. Our newly revised website at www.LaMonacalaw.com also features other books, blogs, video clips, and tools designed to help you navigate the tumultuous waters and treacherous rapids you may encounter in the context of your family law case. We make all these tools available to help our clients find calm waters and move on with a new chart and clear sailing in a way that will radically and positively change their and their families' lives.

Our mission at LaMonaca Law is to provide extra value that goes well beyond the basic representation a client may find at another law firm. We do that with our unique Brutally Honest system, our team approach, and the experiences of our several, multiple-year, award-winning attorneys as highlighted in various magazines. We also have an extensive list of outside resources, experts, and professionals, including our forensic support team and appellate unit. We also employ our VAKOG technology that provides video and audio resources to give clients valuable insights into trial presentation, cutting-edge and imaginative innovation, technology, information, and our personal and professional commitment to the principle and practice known as CANI—constant and never-ending improvement.

To this end, my personal library consists of thousands of books on personal development, psychology, technology, law, innovation, and many other topics. I combine that library with thousands of hours of audio seminars, podcasts, videos, and attendance at some of the most prestigious personal-development seminars throughout the country. I do that to present a fuller picture and a better sense of the ingredients making me who I am, of why the Brutally Honest system was created, and of how LaMonaca Law is prepared and empowered to assist you with your unique family law needs.

Typically, clients call a law firm and make an appointment to meet an attorney for the first time to answer a series of questions about their cases. At LaMonaca Law, before clients ever pick up the phone, they receive information about all aspects of the firm, including videos, blogs, information centers, free full-length books about family law, and many other aids. When they call, they are immediately assigned to attorneys who take time to discuss their issues and begin to learn how best to assist them while providing them with calm assurance that they can help.

In advance of the first meeting, we ask our clients to email us a summary of the facts, issues, and any fears or concerns they have. When a client finally meets us face to face, it's as if we have known each other for some time as we have spoken, reviewed their information, and are ready to hit the ground running. We take whatever time is necessary to provide clients with a road map of the process, educate them on the law and procedures, answer all their questions, and address their fears and concerns. We very commonly spend hours with our clients during these initial meetings. I don't let them leave until I have instilled optimism and confidence in them so they know that even if all others may seem to be against them, we at LaMonaca Law are on their side and are ready to walk hand in hand with them during their journeys.

This book goes beyond that in that I wrote it not just for family law clients but also for all who want to create a better version of themselves and craft a compelling future and legacy for their families.

I thank all my past, current, and future clients, friends, and family who give me the fuel, the passion, and the desire to make a difference in their lives and allow me the privilege of playing a part in creating their compelling futures.

With sincerity and in gratitude,
Gregory P. LaMonaca, Esquire

Disclaimer

The author is not a counselor, psychologist, psychiatrist, financial adviser, accountant, or therapist. Thus, nothing contained within this book should be construed as rendering any medical, psychological, financial, investment, psychiatric, therapeutic, or similar advice. While Mr. LaMonaca is an attorney by trade, nothing in this book should be construed as rendering legal advice. This book should be used for informational purposes only and should not be relied on by the reader as rendering any professional advice. Readers are encouraged to seek professional assistance for advice in any of the above-mentioned categories and beyond.

The information and advice published in this book or made available through the LaMonaca Law or the Brutally Honest website is not intended to replace the services of a physician, counselor, accountant, financial adviser, or lawyer, nor does it constitute a doctor-patient or attorney-client relationship. Information in this book and on the LaMonaca Law and Brutally Honest website is provided for informational purposes only and is not a substitute for professional, medical, or legal advice. You should not use any of this information for diagnosing or treating medical, psychological, or other health conditions.

You should consult a physician in all matters relating to your health and particularly with respect to any symptoms that may require diagnosis or medical attention.

Any action on your part in response to the information provided in this book or on the website is at your discretion. The author of this book makes no representations or warranties with respect to any information offered or provided on or through the LaMonaca Law, Brutally Honest website or this book. The author of this book, LaMonaca Law and the Brutally Honest companies, are not liable for any direct or indirect claim, loss, or damage resulting from use of this book, the Brutally Honest website, LaMonaca Law website, and/or any website(s) linked to it.

A Note on Grammar Revisited

Included in the final version of the previously released *Brutally Honest Life Management Journal* 2009 was a section that was received with humor, levity, and ultimately sincerity. The section was called "A Note on Grammar." Given that the contents as written in 2009 are still equally applicable today, I include once again this oft-mentioned notice.

In creating this product, I have completed countless revisions over many years. As you will see, there are references to various times I was writing this. I left many of the exact dates and examples intact to emphasize the importance of how time changes. Once I created what I believed to be the final version, there soon came another final version followed by the absolute final version, which was eclipsed by yet another update. I have professed to be within days of publishing this book for a long time. The final review was submitted to the editor in 2019 while the first draft of this book dates back several years.

What you learn while writing a book and frankly in life is that there are always ways something can be changed, improved, or modified. In the end, however, a true leader makes decisions that others fear to make. Based on that, what you see in your hands is the result of my decision to push the start button and release this book.

I am not a professional writer with the ability to perfect every sentence. However, I am a visionary with passion, dedication, and an unquenchable thirst to learn and share these lessons with others. By doing that, I have had the privilege to change the lives of countless individuals. What I did do, however, was pay a lot of money to the fine editors of iUniverse to attempt to make my writer's passion grammatically correct. I laugh as I recall the original, red-lined, and marked-up draft of the first book and again here. The editors' revisions turned each page into a sea of red corrections as they did their best to assist me. That said, I am certain that despite their best efforts, readers will find grammatical and spelling errors, syntax problems, format issues, and a whole lot of other big, fancy grammatical terms that no doubt have meaning to others but not to me. If you find errors, that's okay because that will mean you're reading this book and absorbing its meaning.

It is not my goal in releasing this book to go on book tours and win a Pulitzer Prize—or any other awards, for that matter. I am not releasing this book to make a fortune. I get a chuckle each year when I get my IRS statement including my income from the first book. It amounts to literally pennies with each book purchased.

As is the case with life, this book is not perfect. What it is, however, is the result of blood, sweat, and tears I shed during a lifetime of accumulating lessons that have worked for me, my family, clients, and friends. If you apply them, they will change your life. That's this book's purpose.

I apologize to all the wordsmiths out there for insulting their inherent love of the written word, but I hope they get as much out of reading this book as I did writing it.

Acknowledgments

IN LIFE, WE MEET PEOPLE WHO INSPIRE, ENCOURAGE, AND MOTIVATE us. I have been blessed with many such individuals.

To Monica, my best friend and soul mate. She has been by my side since age fourteen. She epitomizes what unconditional love is. She is the most generous, loving, and giving person I know. As a wife, mother, sister, teacher, partner, and companion, she has strode side by side with me at every step. She has devoted her life to helping others while always placing her needs second. I love you forever and a day.

To Alyssa and Gregory. You have grown into such amazing individuals and have made your mother and me very proud. Your zest for life, passion, energy, and respect for others will always serve you well. You have been my inspiration for doing what I do. Continue to make positive ripples in everything you do while having fun on the journey.

To Mom and Dad. As my life has evolved and I have faced many obstacles, the foundation you lovingly gave me has provided the resilience and perseverance I needed to overcome and continue along my path. Thank you for showing me what old-school Italian values are all about.

To Steven and Joey. You have made me proud to be your younger brother. I have learned many lessons from you over the years, and I am grateful for everything you continue to add to my life. You are both successful in your own ways.

To Jim Grim, my brother from another mother and coauthor of the original *Brutally Honest Life Management Journal*. Your strength, courage, and positive attitude inspire me each day. No other has shared as many likes, passions, and family values with me as you did. When you left us, I lost a piece of my soul. I watched you battle for your life over several years. By implementing the warriors' code, you battled to a degree no human could possibly sustain, but you did for so long.

As we spent those precious last weeks together, you echoed over and over God, family, faith, and friends. You lived integrating all these. Our faith tells us we will meet again. Till then, I take solace in knowing that a large piece of you remains a part of me and will help me help others by utilizing the brutally honest principles we practiced and preached. Your impact on this planet is indelible, and your legacy will remain for generations. As I said in my last words to you and so many times before that, I love you, my brother.

I thank my loyal friends and advisers, including Kevin S, Tommy C, Steve Du, Steve R, Chris M, Jim M, Linda M, Steven Do, Bill A, Robert O, Glenn M, Dr. Jean Belasco, Dr. Andrew Bongiovanni, and all of those who have combined to make me who I am.

To all my team members at LaMonaca Law, thank you for your tireless dedication, loyalty, and shared passion to provide a voice for all our clients. You make work fun every day as we share LaMonaca Law's core values that make up our unique culture.

To my many clients past, present, and future. Thank you for providing the inspiration that has fueled me on the journey. With each new challenge, you allow us to join you on your journeys to find unique and compelling futures for you and your families.

Introduction

NEW YEAR'S EVE. WE GET READY TO CELEBRATE THE BEGINNING OF another year with those we love. Millions await the ball dropping at Times Square, and people everywhere celebrate, kiss, embrace, and toast in the New Year. It's a ritual as old as time itself. On this night, at this time, in this moment, all of us unite in this ritual, which tends to make us all feel good and celebrate the now as well as the future. We all enjoy a sense of a new opportunity. All we may have failed to accomplish in the prior year seems neutralized, and we receive a second chance to attain our goals and aim high.

It's a great time that will be a part of our culture forever. As I look in the faces of G and Liss, I wonder what the world will look like when they are my age and are sitting with their children. What's in store for them as technology meets the future? When the future becomes the now? I read voraciously about future technology. Our world today is radically different from the world I lived in when I was their age, and it will be radically different when they are my age. The difference is magnified for them because of the exponential rate of change. What took decades in the past is now taking just years, months, or weeks to change because of the rapidly and ever-evolving technology.

Society comes up with fancy names for each of these generations. The World War II generation was born before 1945, the baby boomers were born between 1946 and 1964, the Generation Xers were born between 1965 and 1977, the Generation Yers—the millennials—were born between 1977 and 1995, and the Generation Zers were born after 1995. What I refer to as Generation Now represents the total of all this collective wisdom.

I am very proud to say that as I write this, LaMonaca Law currently has representation from each generation as follows:

Traditionalists	Over age 71
Baby Boomers	Ages 50–71
Generation X	Ages 38–49
Millennials / Generation Y	Ages 20–38
Generation Z	Under age 20

Respecting what each generation has to offer is at the core of my being and the philosophy I incorporate into my life and the law firm. Understanding what each has to offer allows me to be eclectic in my thinking. With a diversity of political beliefs, religions, and races, we embody a diverse firm that benefits from an eclectic array of knowledge, information, backgrounds, experiences, and beliefs that combine to give our clients representation that incorporates this team effect.

These fancy titles come with reams of data based on study after study of attributes associated with each group. It is nice sometimes to read these studies and see what we are supposed to be like. I enjoy reading these studies, as they are accurate in a global sense and are amusing— akin to reading a horoscope, a novel detour from life that allows us some momentary pleasure.

While I have no problem with any of those types of things, I have little tolerance for those who use them as excuses for why they have not been able to do things. Don't get me wrong—some things of course obviously cannot be attained. Despite my best wishes, I don't see myself playing professional football or flying with the assistance of just my flapping arms. As life evolves from one generation to the next, we will find that our ability to rely on others will slowly go by the wayside and give way to more-individual models.

The team approach baby boomers and Generation X use has devolved to a society that now relies more on the internet, technology, and an increasing demand for immediate satisfaction and instant gratification. With the internet, we are seconds away from getting information that we once would have had to get in a car and drive to a library to get. I recently read that in the near future, the speed of a Google search will be supplanted by nanotechnology that will include robots the size of the head of a pin that will be in our brains. This will allow us to simply think of something and the information will instantly go from our brain to the cloud and download into our brains in a millisecond. Conversations with others will be seamless with infinite information a mere thought away.

In the past few years, we found the closing of Borders bookstores, another casualty of the technological age in which books can be downloaded from the comfort of our homes to our tablets or phones. We can order countless products via our smartphones and have items delivered to us within a day by Amazon and many other online retailers. We will soon have drones delivering items within hours or even minutes. Instant gratification will be demanded, not just requested.

We live in scary times based on the fear of the unknown. If you are secure in life right now and have arrived at your safe destination, good for you. You've done all you were supposed to and can move forward into the unknown wearing armor. But you might not be in this category. Perhaps you've lost your job, have little or no savings, or have no clear direction in life. Maybe you're in a bad relationship or going through a divorce. Perhaps you're fighting a custody battle for your children, are in poor physical health, aren't satisfied with your career path, or fear losing your job due to downsizing prompted by technology. Maybe your skills are outdated, or your employer can now hire a millennial or Generation Xer to do the job you once did quicker, faster, and at half the cost. Have you lost a loved one? Has a friend moved away or lost touch with you?

For those of you who felt good at the beginning of the last paragraph believing you could coast through the future with your suit of armor, don't get too comfortable. Fear, anxiety, depression, desperation, alarm, embarrassment, anger, loss of control, panic—any of these words sound familiar? Do you have other words not on this list?

We just came out of one of the worst economic downturns since the Great Depression and have had a revitalization with the pundits once again talking about a bubble as the stock market has hit new highs. Bitcoins and cryptocurrencies are hot topics. The Depression was something I thought existed only in history books, a time when things were very bad and caused my distant relatives to sell their possessions because they lost their jobs. That was reality back then, but today, we can't fully appreciate what they went through. Many of you reading this are closer to the feelings of that time. Maybe you or your parents lived through it. The closer you are to having lived through the Great Depression, the more powerful the feelings, thoughts, memories, and emotions you have about it. As I review this draft in December 2018, we once again have seen the stock market plummet, causing great fear and anxiety once again. Where it will end, nobody knows. What we know for sure however is that we don't know anything for sure!

Regardless of where you were on the memory scale above, one thing we all have in common is that we all are now living with memories of a time rivaled only by the Great Depression. Depending on when you are reading this, you'll be living in times of amazing economic abundance with a thriving economy or in the middle of another economic collapse. History has been and will be cyclic.

On October 9, 2007, the Dow Jones Industrial Average hit an all-time high of 14,164. By March 2009, it had fallen over 50 percent to 6,469. How could a country that has evolved technologically by leaps and bounds since that time fall again? Most of us unfortunately didn't ask that question. I was taught the basics that have been ingrained in me as far back as I can recall. Show respect to elders, say please and thank you, save money, dollar-cost average, diversify, invest in stocks, invest in real estate, get a good education, be debt free, be ahead of the curve with technology, never stop learning, read and study the greats, mentor others, give back, and work hard. If you do these things, you are almost certain to succeed; they're the basic ingredients of a proven recipe for success. They give you faith and confidence to weather the storms. Those who were able to ride out the storm and continued to buy on the way down as opposed to panic selling were rewarded. On June 28, 2013, the Dow was back at 14,909. In 2016, the fifty-two-week low was 15,451, and the high was 18,668. On March 25, 2017, the Dow closed at 20,596.

As I edit this on New Year's Eve in 2017, the Dow finished one the greatest years in its history closing at 24,719. By the first week of February 2018, the Dow's meteoric rise eclipsed 26,500. Guess what? Just two months later, after incredible volatility, on April 6, 2018, the Dow was at

23,932. Panic? Fear? That's the glass half empty. An incredible buying opportunity? That's the glass half full.

When will it end? No one knows. Or do they? Just as quickly as I wrote the last paragraph, as the week ended on February 9, 2018, the market sunk quicker than any time in history; it lost more than 12 percent in a matter of days with 1,000-plus-point swings to close the week at 24,190. It was actually much lower yesterday, but it closed the week on an upswing. Throughout 2018 the market rose again to all time high's, only to plummet at the end of the year with the Nasdaq and S&P falling into bear market territory (a fall of over 20% from its high), and the Dow Jones Industrial Average very close. On this Christmas Eve, December 24, 2018, doom and gloom was everywhere, making it the worst Christmas Eve in history. The Dow is now at 22,445.37, the Nasdaq is at 6332.39 and the S&P 500 is at 2,416.62. OK, do we conclude that the market is crashing? Are we heading into a recession? Should we panic even more? Well, the very next trading day, December 26, 2018, after the close of the market, the headlines read, "Dow logs biggest daily point gain ever," as it surged 1,086.25 points.

For most investors, it was a time of panic. For me, it was a time of opportunity. I described it as returns after Christmas, when many people return gifts they had bought at full price. That's when I'm buying them at reduced prices. You will learn this entire process and strategy in several chapters of this book. No one can predict the highs or lows of the market. What you can do, however, is create a proactive mind-set so not if, but when, these times come, you will be well prepared to implement your well-thought-out plan. Stay tuned.

When do you buy? When do you sell? Should I panic and sell everything, or will the increase we have been seeing for years continue? No matter how you look at it, however, those were/are scary times. The only true answer is that no one has the answers. You can, however, learn techniques to create your own, panic-free approach. You will learn real-life examples of this in this book.

What went wrong that caused these epic drops? The answer to that is the reason for the words used in the opening sentence. Millions of people throughout the world had age-old beliefs turned around overnight. These beliefs were as strong for me as my belief that if I drop a rock out a window, it'll fall. Will it, though? I don't know anymore. Most people I speak with and mentor describe a numbness they felt when the market collapsed seemingly overnight. It brings back memories of Mr. Freeze in the Batman series. He would hit his opponents with his freeze ray and they would be frozen in time. That's a great way of describing many clients I represent and the family and friends I mentor. They can see everything that is happening but feel frozen or helpless because they don't know what to do to help themselves.

As I was editing an earlier draft of this book before sending it to the publisher, on December 28, 2017, the Dow had once again made an all-time high and ended one of the greatest years in history at 24,803. Having lived through these radical ups and downs, I love seeing once again all the groups that take credit for this all-time high. Politicians from both sides take credit for the strong economy. The reality is what I used to shout to my kids when we were riding roller coasters and ascending the first steep hill: "What goes up must come down!" Will those who were hit hard financially just a few short years ago learn their lesson this time? Will they be prepared and prepare their families? Will they learn from the past, analyze the present, and plan for the future? Most won't, but you will. Those who don't will again convince themselves that this time is different because they have newfound knowledge and that the increase in their portfolios was due to their great skills. They will be met with future decimation once again as their misplaced confidence will see them hit bottom. This year thus far through December 2018 has seen this unfold in real time. Catastrophic highs followed by deep declines and corrections. Extreme euphoria earlier in the year followed by panic stricken results at other times.

As I originally wrote this paragraph, the Republican National Convention was wrapping up. They nominated Donald Trump as their choice to run for president. The Democrats assembled in Philadelphia for their convention, where Hillary Clinton was nominated as their choice. Donald Trump went on to win a riveting and controversial presidency. The first two years of his presidency has been riddled with issues, contention, and polarization throughout the country. But this book is not about politics; it's about learning and implementing techniques that can help everyone regardless of his or her personal preferences. I hope we can become a nation in which we can come together and respectfully and peacefully express and share our beliefs, learn and grow together, and keep our citizens, children, and future generations safe. You will learn techniques in this book to thrive regardless of the many obstacles life will present now and in the future.

As far as safety, as I write this, our world is in epic crisis. Attacks by terrorists plague the world; each day brings more stories of mass killings, shootings, and bombings. The United States has experienced mass shootings all over the country; mass terrorist attacks have invaded our soil and put people in fear. Issues between races have increased from peaceful citizens on both sides adhering to our American rights of free speech and assembly to groups spawning extremists that have taken things to a new level by intentionally inciting riots and making deliberate calls to kill others. Attacks on various leaders, bombs sent in the mail, horrific anti-sematic attacks on a Pittsburgh Synagogue all add to the fear and strife in the World.

I believe strongly in protecting all the rights we have in the Unites States. As you will see, I respect all groups' right to peacefully protest and passionately pursue their beliefs. As Americans, we need different opinions to have a system of checks and balances that will allow us all to hear others' views, understand why some think differently, and perhaps incorporate others' views into our own. I think the vast number of people on either side of an issue are passionate but peaceful. On the extremes, we will always have simply bad people who commit crimes, abuse their positions, and are bad reflections of the groups they represent. I hope we can continue to come together on common ground and coexist as Americans while understanding and learning from each other and respect others' rights to peaceful beliefs. I have dedicated my life to being passionate about my beliefs while learning and growing through the absorption of information from many other points of view.

Depending on whom you listen to, the divorce rate hovers between 50 and 55 percent nationwide. Countless clients come to me shocked, depressed, and feeling helpless. They want solutions to their problems.

It's a role I take very seriously; it fuels me every day. Thankfully, there is hope for all of them, a way to break out of the frozen tundra and move forward. Through the Brutally Honest system, I can make a difference in my clients' and their children's lives and give them hope for the future. Each client is different; they all seek different solutions. It could be that they want a divorce, want custody of their children, want to relocate to another state or country, have been abused by their spouses, have had their children abducted to another state or country, and a myriad of other problems. They too find themselves asking, Why?

When I have my first meetings with clients, they usually say at some point that they know for sure that their spouses or exes will or will not act in certain ways as we move forward in the representation. They are sure that they will not pursue primary custody and will continue to pay the bills. They firmly state, "He said I could remain in the house indefinitely" and many other absolute statements. On the one hand, they come to me for advice, guidance, and a plan to guide them through this most emotional and fearful time in their lives. My question to them when they respond this way is, "When you said 'I do' many years ago on that most happy day of your marriage, did you ever think you'd be in a family lawyer's office in the future seeking a divorce?" They look at me blankly. Their voices become shallow. Their body language slows, and they solemnly say, "No." They then release themselves to the process and leave open the possibility that change is possible.

They took the critical first step toward positively changing their and their children's lives. To them, bricks no longer fall when released from a second-story window. They are numb and cannot fathom how they wound up in this position. Through the Brutally Honest system, we begin finding out how this occurred and more important, why it occurred, so as we devise a path forward for them, we can use the past as our guide. We then provide them with resources to help them through their current pain and assist them in developing a clear, concise, and compelling future for themselves and their children. This sense of clarity gives them a sense of peace and serenity as they learn to accept the reality of their situation while giving them a vivid vision of a good future.

At LaMonaca Law, we utilize a team approach that allows us to match a client's unique facts, budget, and wishes with a custom-designed team that best matches their needs. The entire firm along with our resources and diverse and collective knowledge increase their comfort level and gives them assurance; we have the ability to best serve each client's unique needs.

As I write this, the number of new clients coming into the firm is at an all-time high. When I meet with new clients, I get the opportunity to make a difference in their lives and give them the tools and strength they need to address extremely emotional and scary issues, including their fears and concerns; I map out a way to their compelling futures. Due to time constraints, costs, and budgets, I do not have the pleasure of meeting or representing every client in the firm. I can, however, expose each of them to the Brutally Honest system by and through the other attorneys and team members in the firm with whom I meet to collectively share and exchange knowledge, cutting-edge law, technology, and the Brutally Honest system. I also get to share the Brutally Honest system through my books, videos, blogs, our website, and updates to our Facebook page and many other social-media sites.

At LaMonaca Law, we practice what we preach. At the end of each year, I personally conduct one-on-one meetings with each team member; we take hours to review not just their goals, but also their passions, interests, and objectives. I then go back and have additional three- to four-hour-long meetings with each of my leadership team members. When I'm done, I have over fifty hours of additional knowledge to better serve our clients and team members. We each leave with newfound vision, passion, and purpose.

As bad as the last decade has been with the myriad of ups and downs we have experienced, there always lies within each of us a fear of the unknown, the future. Are we out of the fog yet? Is there another economic tornado in our path? Will the current economic boom continue? The answer to this is simple, isn't it? Just read the papers, listen to the radio, and watch the many financial TV shows. They have the answers, right? Well, if you relied on most of their advice in the last few years, you would be exactly where you are now.

This time around is different though, right? I think not. If you spent one day writing down what each of the many different experts say about the economy and their advice this time around, you would find radically different ideas, beliefs, and suggestions. If you weren't confused before you began listening, you no doubt would be when you finished doing that.

In the winter of 2016, we were again in the beginning stages of the presidential election with all the typical banter. So how were we doing? That's easy. According to all the Democratic pundits, we were doing great. President Obama did an amazing job, so his endorsement of Hillary Clinton for president should be adopted. Everything that was going wrong was based on factors beyond his control. On the other side, the Republicans were fighting among themselves to see who would run against Hillary Clinton. Donald Trump, an incredible long shot just months before, had systematically knocked out every Republican rival. Of course, they all agreed that President Obama and the Democrats had not lived up to any of their promises and the economy and all other problems were because of that. Of course, we needed to elect a Republican president.

What we know for sure, however, is that between now and then, on any given day, depending on who you listen to, you will hear every possible outcome, conspiracy theories, and bad-mouthing on both sides that causes mass confusion. As I am reviewing the draft of this book on October 1, 2016, we are little over a month away from knowing who the next president will be. By the time you are reading this, we will know.

The fun part of a book is that it takes years to finish. As mentioned earlier, on this review date, October 30, 2018, we are wrapping up year two of President Trump's first term. Different date, different polarizing themes, fighting on both sides. It's easy to get lost in all the infighting, controversy, and strong beliefs. In the end, you must make the best decision for you and your family.

While I find this all very fascinating and must admit I do follow all the above as well as listen to and view all these pundits, I know I'll be the same person when I wake up tomorrow morning. That includes the day after each election. I still have the ultimate power to control whom I believe, whom and what I listen to, and what I will do that day to personally change my world, family, friends, clients, and everyone I have the pleasure of meeting that day. My daily mantra always is this—focus on what you can control and disregard what you cannot. It starts initially with taking personal accountability and owning your problems and circumstances.

One of my favorite quotes is by James Allen: "Circumstances don't make the man; they reveal him." Unless and until we take personal accountability for our actions and our circumstances, we will never be prepared for the next generation and certainly will not be able to confront whatever dilemma we may find ourselves in. No, while we may not be able to control some things such as health issues, old age, downsizing, stock market conditions, and so on, we can control how we react to these things and what we will do as a result. While it would be great to be dealt an ace and a jack in every hand of blackjack, reality just doesn't work that way. In life as in blackjack, we are dealt cards randomly, and it's up to us to hold, double down, hit, or fold. Having this control does not guarantee successful outcomes, but it certainly increases our odds of success. The results of our decision to hit with an ace and a jack would be radically different from those who held.

So how do we navigate these tumultuous times with infinite choices? The answer is simple, right? We're in the technology age. We can simply google the answer or ask Alexa or Siri, right? Anything we need is a few clicks or a voice command away.

Maybe as you are reading this—years after I wrote it—you are actually using the nanotechnology mentioned above. Go ahead. Try it. Do a Google search for an answer to whatever problem you have. I know for sure that you will find answers, an endless list of possible solutions, products, books, seminars, and countless other options and opinions. What do you do? How do you make sense of all that? Before movies became on demand, there was Blockbuster. Remember that? You wandered the aisles searching for the perfect movie for that evening, and finally, you'd choose two or three and hope at least one would live up to your expectations.

Today, the internet is a million-movie store we can browse sitting at home, but even that can be paralyzing; we might not know where to begin and thus try some search terms. But then the results can seem infinite, in conflict with each other, and confusing. One author or a site says that the wall is white while another equally well-credentialed source says it's black. You stare at the screen more confused than before.

When clients first meet with me, they are often doing so at the pinnacle of fear, anxiety, and often depression. The area of family law is riddled with emotion. It takes an extremely exceptional person to work in this area. While having an extensive knowledge of the law is of course needed, having the ability to empathize, be compassionate, listen, and turn on a dime to immediately address a client's existing needs is not optional but essential. When I interview potential attorneys and other team members, I review their educations and grades of course, but what's more important is whether I believe they have the full package, which includes all the emotional intelligence traits listed above in addition to legal knowledge.

I do not hire LaMonaca Law team members. We all do … literally. We look through all resumes to narrow the search, and I meet with those we select initially. I tell them to go anywhere in any of our three buildings, walk in on any of my team members, ask any questions they want to, come back, and tell me what they learned about the LaMonaca Law culture. After they leave, I ask my team members what they thought of the candidates. We then set up additional interviews with my individual team leaders followed by group interviews during which multiple team members meet with the candidates. I elicit feedback from everyone so we can collectively decide who would best fit into our LaMonaca Law core culture. Once hired, they go through a comprehensive training program to maximize their effectiveness. While there are never guarantees about the future of any new team member, this process has proven to increase the likelihood of success.

This is why I tell each client that while I cannot guarantee the results, I can guarantee our efforts. More than anything, clients are looking to lose their fear and gain hope for the future. We often take over many cases a month in which our clients have had one, two, or more attorneys. These clients are often upset about their past representation and are often quite vocal about it. While there may be much truth in their emotions and beliefs, we focus on what if anything we can do differently, find the right direction to take, and move in that direction. Often, we find that their current attorneys are doing exactly what we would do. In such cases, we encourage the clients to stay their courses and discuss their concerns with their attorneys.

In such cases that we do accept, I refuse to badmouth their former attorneys—I never take that bait. I'm blessed to work alongside some of the finest family law attorneys on the planet, and we practice in an area of law that's not for everyone. The Brutally Honest system was created to address this very unique type of law. Over the years, the system expanded within the firm as it went from me and my wife, Monica, decades ago to one of the largest family law firms in the area. As the years passed, the Brutally Honest system kept morphing exponentially as we hired each additional attorney, paralegal, legal assistant, bookkeeper, case aid, and intern.

At the beginning, Monica and I did everything out of a spare bedroom in our twin home in Ridley Township, Pennsylvania, until we rented our first office in Media, Pennsylvania, and hired our first part-time paralegal. In the early days, with Monica's assistance, I played every conceivable role; no job was too unimportant.

We evolved over the years; we rented a floor in a building down the street and hired some part-time attorneys. Then we expanded to two floors with additional staff. Over the years, I was honored by several different magazines and ranking services as one of the top family law attorney on the Main Line and the top family law attorney many times. Feature stories were written about me, our team, and the Brutally Honest system.

We ultimately purchased our flagship office on State Street in Media, and two years later, we purchased two buildings on Pearl and Front Streets. Each building houses a separate team with a team leader, several other attorneys, paralegals, and support staff. While our physical office is in Delaware County, Pennsylvania, we are a multicounty Main Line firm having equal amounts of cases in the neighboring Chester and Montgomery Counties. We also have cases in counties throughout Pennsylvania and internationally.

To instill hope in our clients, I acknowledge that as they initially sit in front of me riddled with fear of the present and the future, I ask them to leave open a possibility. My passion is to continuously research, read, and review multiple sources on ways to better serve our clients. My focus is also in the future seeing what cutting-edge things can better help each of our clients. I research other areas outside law that have solved problems in way the traditional legal system has not embraced. I am obsessed with the Japanese concept of *kaizen*—constant improvement. I instill this additional knowledge in my family, friends, team members, clients, and everyone else I can reach.

The practice of law has age-old beliefs that have frozen some practitioners and have made many unwilling to change or challenge these mores, beliefs, and traditions supposedly set in stone. I have also seen many of the country's leading and oldest firms undergoing layoffs if not outright closure during economic downturns. That's led of course to infighting and the departure of partners, associates, and employees not to mention the sorrow all that involves.

I remember going to the offices of a large firm—dozens and dozens of attorneys and staff—for a deposition. And I remember going to the same place later and not seeing that walnut desk in the reception area. I didn't even see a receptionist. A sign told me to push a button for help. The attorney I had come to see came out, and we walked to the conference room for our meeting past as many as thirty empty offices with chairs stacked on desks. That once-prominent, well-respected, old-school law firm was a shell of its former self.

In the months and years that followed, and despite being in the middle of one of the worst economic times in history, LaMonaca Law continued to expand and thrive. I was receiving resumes from attorneys desperately willing to accept a legal secretary position. Those were troubled times in the legal profession and the world.

We consider LaMonaca Law the anti–law firm in that while we respect the history and traditions of the law, we focus more on incorporating that respect with the very real need to change with times and understand the future. Through a combination of these, we have created a firm well equipped to address the unique needs of all our clients. That's the Brutally Honest system.

Being willing to challenge age-old traditions is at the heart of what it takes to change the world in a positive way. That requires total commitment to leaving open the very real probability that what we think we know is not necessarily true. It means to believe there are or can be cures for diseases, improvements in the economy, ways to improve our lives and create abundance, to find our true soul-mate, to improve relations among different societies and cultures, to end starvation, to extend our life spans, and a whole host of things that before today we thought were impossible or never thought of. How do we get from here to there? Let's look at some examples.

Music media has evolved; just think of the progression from 78, 45, and 33 1/3 rpm records, to eight tracks, to cassettes, to CDs, to MP3s, to instant, on-demand iTunes and to Amazon's Echo, with which all I do now is mention the song I want to hear. Where will be next year? Ten years from now?

It's the same thing with computers; something that filled a whole room has been replaced by extremely more powerful and sophisticated devices that are about the size of a very small suitcase and are getting smaller daily. I recently read that the latest IPhone has more power than the first computer that Steve Job's created. What will be the state of computing next year? Ten years from now?

Think of how transportation has evolved from horse and buggy to driverless cars. Entertainment has progressed from Vaudeville stage acts through black-and-white and color movies to instant, on-demand movie services. And virtual reality entertainment is already here.

Consider the evolution medicine has undergone. Leeches, bloodletting, and tribal elders gave way to doctors who made house calls, penicillin, and MRIs. Now, you can have appointments with doctors over the computer no matter where you or they are.

Within the law, there likewise has been an evolution. As is the case with the modalities above, clients also want more value, options, and immediate gratification. Most firms still work on the premise that a client contacts the firm during normal business hours and a secretary not authorized to give any information sets up an appointment later in the week for the client to meet with an attorney. The attorney, typically all dressed up, meets with the client and collects information based on some standard forms meant to handle all clients. If the firm is hired, the representation goes through similar checklists as the case migrates from start to finish. The mighty lawyers sitting on a high perch tell the clients, "Do what I say and you'll be fine."

At LaMonaca Law, it's not unusual for a client to email me in the middle of the night and get a response seconds later. I kid you not. As I was writing this section from my home office on a Saturday afternoon, my phone, which is linked to our office phone system, rang. "Hello. This is Greg LaMonaca." Silence for a few beats … "I can't believe you answered the phone!" I spent fifteen minutes with this new client answering questions that eased her anxiety and allowed her to peacefully get through her weekend. She later became a client.

This past week saw over a dozen requests come through outside regular business hours by phone, email, requests through our website and our instant chat feature online, and so on. All those who called or emailed received what they needed—answers to things that were worrying them and the lessening of their fear. All our team members from front desk to attorneys are empowered to address questions about typical costs, retainers, processes, and the like. Not every caller becomes a client, but they all get to interact with us through our many different communication vehicles to get instant answers that alleviate their fears and concerns right away. They then make an informed decision about what's best for them and their families.

Existing and potential clients can also view online videos, photos, bios of myself and other team members, read cutting-edge articles and blogs written by our team members, and immediately download for free from www.lamonacalaw.com one of my latest books, *The Brutally Honest Pennsylvania Divorce & Custody Survival Guide (Note: to be updated in early 2019 to include the financial aspects of divorce, and to be titled "The Brutally Honest Pennsylvania Divorce, Custody & Financial Survival Guide")*. This seventy-plus page book is packed with information about many areas of Pennsylvania family law, about who we are and how we go about representing clients, and many other useful tools. This immediate and free source provides people with timely, added-value information that can further address their questions, fears, and concerns before ever having to speak to me or other team members, and they can do so in the privacy of their homes. Once they do so and choose to make an appointment, they come in many steps ahead of individuals who proceed under the old-school way of doing things. Our clients can utilize Face Time, Skype, audio and video conferencing, and other media that allow us to present what we do in a format that best matches their preferences and learning styles.

So where will the practice of law be next year and ten years from now? I envision the technology we mentioned above continuing to improve exponentially. The ability of clients to instantly communicate will expand to incorporate the newest and latest technology. I envision the overloaded court system will alleviate their caseloads by allowing video appearances. I imagine a case going forward in which the judge may be in his chambers in one county on video with a witness in another state or country on the same video screen, attorneys for each party at their offices or homes with their clients either at their side, on video, or also at another location. At the push of a button, all involved will be able to see each other on one screen and hear each other as the proceeding is recorded and stored in the cloud as the official court transcription.

I believe all of the above will be enhanced by each of them putting on a virtual reality headset; they will see each other in the same virtual courtroom with few, if any, visceral differences from actually being there.

I and many of my team members recently won a portion of the longest and most expensive cases dealing with false allegations of abuse, protection from abuse, and custody. After many months and seven court appearances with several experts and severe weather—ice and snowstorms—all causing delay, the matter finally resolved one of the parts of the case dealing with protection from abuse. If the abovementioned technology was available or should I say allowable—and it is available— the case could have been done much more efficiently and cost effectively and would have allowed it to be resolved in a much timelier fashion.

From the court's end, such a system would reduce the ever-increasing backlog of cases, more efficiently allow judges to manage their lists, create less of a need for duplicative staffing, and allow for quicker resolution of cases. Supplementary professions such as psychology, accounting, counseling, and many others can and should follow suit with appropriate changes that will embrace the newest and latest technology.

This type of progression would of course involve a detailed analysis and potential change of long-standing legal, ethical, and moral constraints. Any worthwhile change will naturally entail an evaluation in the way things have been done and the reasons for doing so, the current effect of the way things are done, a consideration of alternative methods, and a weighing of the costs and benefit of changing.

I for one have been at the forefront for this change and believe that the benefits current and future technology will provide us will far outweigh any negatives. Laws have always been changed, eliminated, or modified to meet the evolving demands of society. In these events, there are often exploratory or advisory boards comprising an array of individuals who advise the legislature on the best way incorporate these changes. I have every confidence that insofar as implementing my suggested changes and others, the same prudent mechanisms can be implemented to ensure that change occurs and ethics remain.

Ray Kurzweil and Peter Diamandis, founders of Singularity University, are at the forefront of this futuristic technology. Diamandis was featured in the several editions of *Success* magazine. He founded XPRIZE, which awards multimillions of dollars to the creators of groundbreaking technologies. Diamandis stated, "In keeping with that goal, the XPRIZE model is simple and beautifully empowering. It searches for problems that require a breakthrough solution—something so far off, so daft, that even approaching it requires a wholesale rejection of past thinking" in areas such as space exploration, DNA mapping, education apps, ocean-floor mapping, robotic-floor exploration, and human longevity. If he is successful, there will be a time when we could see age 100 being half our average life span. Diamandis wants technology in many areas to become as widely available as air travel is today. And not too long ago, that would've been a ridiculous forecast.

As part of my constant quest for additional skills and knowledge, I read articles like those above, have read several of his books, Ray Kurzweil's books, and thousands of other books that keep me not only current but futuristic. I listen to podcasts daily, listen to audiobooks, attend seminars, watch online seminars, watch YouTube videos, meet with like-minded individuals, ask countless questions of family, friends, and clients and many other sources that fuel my passion to change, make a difference, and bring cutting-edge technology to LaMonaca Law, my life, and the lives of my family, friends, and clients; that's fun, different, and transformative. I interact with others with the total of this information. How can it not give me and everyone I share this knowledge with an edge? My obsession has evolved and is growing and expanding. It's become part of my subconscious, and it allows me to act, react, and speak with others seamlessly.

So how do you make sense out of our tumultuous and ever-changing world? How do you know where to begin? I believe there is a path back to the right direction, one that I can personally attest works. The path I've been on is at times rocky, scary, and riddled with obstacles, but it has etched in me core beliefs that have positively impacted my life and those of my wife, children, family, team members, friends and countless clients I have represented using this formula. Like life, no formula or plan is perfect or guaranteed. It will not work for everyone all the time, and it takes ongoing effort. I know for sure, however, that if you do not leave the starting line of a race, you'll never get to the finish line.

You will find in this book real solutions that have allowed me to put on running shoes, appear at the starting line, get a quick jump on my competition when I heard the starter pistol, stay laser focused on the finish line, develop momentum as the race progressed, anticipated the hurdles on the track, leaped over each, regrouped when I periodically stumbled, developed the mind-set to stick to my plan, and ultimately cross the finish line. I learned to shake hands with all the others in the race and thank them for challenging me and to praise God, my family, friends, and mentors who helped me prepare for and run the race. I give these real solutions to the Now Generation so they can carry the baton and change the world in their unique styles.

The process I will describe requires a considerable amount of effort, a work ethic, and a steadfast determination on the part of those who implement it, but it is not overwhelming because it requires only small, incremental, daily steps. If that's done consistently, over time, radical change will take place. I provide those I mentor, guide, and represent a GPS system that lets them glimpse their future if they stay the course. They define their courses, their destination, and I provide the role of accountability partner to guide them and provide advice and resources as tools they can use in their journeys.

The difference between this system and others is that the destinations people take will be generated and guided by them. While they rely on resources and information, they determine what their target is, not author A or mentor B. But I repeat that this process takes work. Many people have asked me for help in guiding them; I took the time to give them advice I knew could help them only to find several months later that they come back complaining about the same problem and seeking my help again. When I ask them if they had followed my advice, they stammer excuses about why they did not or could not. I politely tell them that there is no genie in a bottle that will magically fix all their problems. Effort combined with persistence, passion, and a plan is the way to achieve goals.

If you are looking for a get-rich-quick scheme, you have the wrong book. Brutally Honest is a system designed to combat traditional self-help programs by being realistic—which has the word *real* at its core. I wrote this to give you a radically different approach to not only surviving in this new world but sur-thriving.

Wherever you find yourself in life right now, this book will help you design a plan to get to your personal next level, to provide you with a level of empowerment, and provide you and your family with a compelling future. Once there, you—not the world or fate—will be in control of your destiny.

You may be in a fantastic place in your life, or you may feel hopeless. Everyone has that next level he or she is seeking. Some people might want to learn how to become financially secure while others are looking for pain relief, solutions to their marital difficulties, a greater sense of peace and calm, or perhaps a better connection with their religion and families.

Some seek reconciliation with estranged friends or ways to achieve any one of thousands of personal aspirations. We all have something we'd like to improve. It starts with acknowledging we can improve, taking that critical first step, being open to the possibility that their really may be a solution, writing down the options, determining what resources we have, and begin monitoring the process and progress toward what we want to achieve or change. Regardless of our pasts and our futures, we all have the present, the now. With that comes a new set of possibilities and solutions. What we do with this moment in time is up to us.

The fact that you're reading this book tells me you are different and are committed to being successful and making ongoing, positive changes in your life and those of your family and friends. For this, I honor you, and I thank you for allowing me into your life.

It has been my life's passion to research and learn from countless authors, lecturers, family, friends, clients, and many other sources mentioned above and later in this book. It is my honor and pleasure to share this knowledge with each of you in hopes that you too may find joy and peace in whatever outcome you desire. Welcome to Generation Now!

SECTION 1
THE JOURNEY

Chapter 1

What Is Brutally Honest?

BRUTALLY HONEST IS THE SUM OF THE AUTHORS' EXPERIENCES, WORK, passion, and obstacles that they collectively overcame. The system evolved in my law firm as a way to assist my clients to develop plans to get through a myriad of emotional, physical, economic, and straight-out fearful roadblocks in their paths sometimes put there by others and other times self-imposed.

My personal journey found me having to develop many resources and solutions to the various physical obstacles in my path as I chronicled in the first book, *Brutally Honest Life Management Journal* 2009. In it, I provided verbatim text from my personal journal from when I was paralyzed in 2005. I documented each day of my recovery process. On my journey, I read thousands of articles and books, listened to and viewed self-help programs, and attended countless seminars and the like. By availing myself of endless ideas, plans, processes, resources, and suggestions from some of the most influential individuals from the beginning of time to the present, I added daily to my knowledge and resource base. By modeling these great leaders, I replicated many of the outstanding results they achieved. While I may not have always agreed with each source and its suggestions, I was slowly developing a deep pit of ideas that I could use and share with family, friends, and clients.

These books, CDs, and seminars gave me tools to use and pass on to others that helped us overcome many barriers in our paths. I'd find myself listening to a client relaying a problem he or she was facing, and my brain—with absolute clarity and mastery and at warp speed—would come up with solutions that had been ingrained in my brain one by one as I read, listened to, or processed information over the years from these books, audios, and seminars. I would render advice to my clients in the form of suggestions and guidance based on similar obstacles that countless authors, lecturers, clients, and speakers had overcome.

I combine my doctor of law degree with information I obtained while achieving my doctor of life degree. Much as a doctor's prescription does not always work and needs to be changed, I too give the best advice I know based on the problems my clients present with while realizing the initial plan is never guaranteed to work. It takes development, monitoring, adjusting, and a clear and compelling vision of where you want to end up. The likelihood of success increases as the trust, bond, and rapport between myself and my clients increase. We become a team heading down the path to achieve their goals.

Through this system, I had the pleasure of meeting one of the closest friends in my life, James Grim. Jim came to me many years ago to assist him with a custody matter and related family law matters. I require my clients to write a detailed journal indicating their past and where they are presently and outlining their goals. When I first met Jim and told him about my studies and beliefs and encouraged him to also read self-help books, he looked at me as if I had three heads; he didn't believe any of that. But in working with Jim over the following months and then years, I realized he and I were kindred spirits. He was a passionate self-starter who shared my insatiable appetite for knowledge. He was one of the most caring fathers I knew; he had given up millions of dollars in potential income to pursue a fulfilling life with his two wonderful daughters and his wife, Cyndii. He was a brilliant entrepreneur who was one of the few people who could motivate me and push me to higher levels. He and Cyndii built from the ground up one of the most successful and amazing salons on the Main Line, Ultimate Image Salon and Spa (ultimateimagesalon.com).

Over the years as his legal case evolved, so did our friendship. After the case was closed, we began meeting more frequently. We'd get together and share our blessings and hurdles. We'd talk about how the many people we studied had changed the world. We'd constantly challenge each other to improve mentally, physically, and spiritually. He and I would share hundreds of self-improvement books, audios, and seminars. We would discuss plans to individually—and later together—change the world.

Over time, we decided to incorporate all this information in a brand that would encompass this philosophy and unique style of law. That was how Brutally Honest started taking shape. We figured that if this system has worked so well in my family law practice to help individuals overcome some very difficult situations, it could help others outside the family law context overcome their obstacles. Thus Brutally Honest evolved.

Over the following years, the system my law firm used was written out and incorporated into a three-step system. In 2009, Jim and I collaborated on *The Brutally Honest Life Management Journal*.

Jim and I served as each other's accountability partner. We discussed our lives, businesses, goals, dreams, and ambitions. Our dinner meetings every other week evolved into much more. We would share a bottle of wine, eat sushi, and philosophize about all the above topics and life's many wonderful opportunities and challenges. As the wine flowed, so did the topics. We didn't simply agree with each other and share successes; we challenged each other's ideas and held each other accountable to what we said we would do; the feedback we gave each other was brutally honest. At times, our meetings became heated; we'd challenge each other's excuses for why something hadn't gotten done. What always existed at the core, however, was an unconditional friendship that made us feel secure enough to challenge each other and speak honestly and openly about our insecurities, vulnerabilities, and feelings.

We were each other's accountability partner; we wanted the other to achieve. How many so-called friends do you have tell you they want the best for you but consciously or subconsciously hope you fail so they can feel better about themselves? Jim was a true crusader for my life, and I always strived to be that for him.

Out of these meetings came another book we collaborated on entitled *Thursdays with Greg and Jim*, an engaging look into our biweekly meetings during which we reviewed topics that we had discussed and worked through in our lives that can now help others. Stay tuned.

At the core of all of this, the Brutally Honest process evolved through my law firm and my practice of assisting individuals get through their highly emotional and often tumultuous family law situations. Dedicated, wonderful parents, spouses, and children wake up finding themselves in the middle of life-altering situations; some know what the cause is, but more often, they don't. What seem obvious to others looking from the outside in at the person in the eye of the storm is not always obvious to that person.

My initial task is to give them a mechanism to begin getting through their storms, seeing more clearly, and analyzing their past to determine what went well and what had not. I require my clients to give me a detailed journal going back to the beginning of the relationship to the present. This has been the cornerstone of my practice and the Brutally Honest system. It allows clients to give me details about their cases that will allow me to best represent them. It also acts as a much-needed catharsis as perhaps for the first time, the clients have detailed in depth the origins of their problems; that plants the seeds of their new, compelling futures.

This process of going backward is called the breakdown stage. In this first step, clients narrowing in on, define, and create a clear and concise picture of what they need, not what society says they need. In this look backward, they reach deep levels of their being, their souls core. They can then make decisions for themselves and their families with clear minds. Often, they will shed tears as they take this most critical first step.

In step two, individuals develop their Brutally Honest Target Zones—personal goals they set for the various categories of their lives. Only when they reach their Souls Core are they finally alone with themselves, their thoughts, and their feelings; they can then shed all societal input and pressure and define what truly matters to them.

In step three, the journey begins toward attaining their Brutally Honest Target Zones where they use the information they gained in step one to guide them along the path. Whatever went well will be replicated, and whatever didn't will be avoided. Of course, the journey must be carefully monitored as the individual moves forward. I require my clients to submit ongoing updates to their journals. Through this process, I can assist them in staying on track; if they hit inevitable hurdles, we can quickly adjust course. The Brutally Honest process has radically transformed the lives of countless individuals and continues to be the cornerstone of my practice, my life, and my world.

As I mentioned earlier, this book was written over several years. As I was editing the last section, I did so with great remorse and pain. On February 13, 2017, this world lost one of the greatest individuals I have ever known. My brother Jim lost his third battle with cancer. He taught me as much in his last days as he did in the many years prior. The void left in my life is indescribable. He is simply irreplaceable. It is my hope that through this book and all I do, I will be able to continue to honor and share his legacy.

Chapter 2

Taking Action

THE SECOND YOU DECIDE TO MAKE A CHANGE IN YOUR LIFE, YOU TAKE action. When you started reading this book, you took significantly more action. Utilizing the tools in this book and moving forward toward your goals is accelerated action, something you must strive for.

We all start with a general premise that we want to succeed, we want better lives for ourselves and our families, we want to achieve our goals, and we want to be more physically active and in great shape and have an unlimited list of personal goals. But achieving these things is not as easy as simply wishing, hoping, or dreaming to do so. Whatever is on your list, you must at some point, take action that starts you along your path toward achieving it. What's holding you back?

Why wouldn't we all simply take immediate action to attain what we want and need? It could be that our goal may simply not be compelling enough to make us want to take action. We may decide consciously or subconsciously that the journey to a particular goal will give us less pleasure than the status quo is.

Let's assume you decide you want to be in excellent health and lose a few pounds. Picture yourself arriving home on a Friday night after a particularly grueling workweek, relaxing in your favorite recliner, and enjoying a warm, calming fire. Imagine eating your favorite food as you watch your favorite TV show. You're relaxed. Then you see a commercial that shows an ultra-fit individual performing the newest exercise program and telling you it's time to get off the couch and partake in their grueling exercise program that is guaranteed to transform your body and make you healthier. You know you should get off the chair, put down the food, and immediately begin the program, but do you? Why not? You opt for the pleasure of your current state over the pain of exercising right then.

On the other hand, imagine sitting in your recliner and hearing a loud crash followed by the scream of your child in the other room. You immediately jump up and rush to investigate, right? The pain associated with not taking action far outweighs the pleasure of remaining seated. We make thousands of such decisions each day. We systematically process, evaluate, and decide on how to react typically without thinking.

How does this process work? How can we possibly engage in this type of detailed analysis thousands of times a day? That seems impossible; there simply isn't enough time to do this. Or is there? We don't stop to analyze every situation that demands our immediate attention. We make decisions in nanoseconds all day long. We are constantly and immediately making millions of decisions from the time we awake till the time we go to sleep and while we sleep for that matter.

Readers of the *Brutally Honest Life Management Journal* know the answer—the reticular activating system—RAS—of our brains. Simply put, your RAS is your mind's supercomputer with infinite memory, and it has a built-in GPS. This computer is internalizing billions of bits of data and information 24-7. This data is conscious when you read a book for example. As you are reading this sentence right now, your eyes are scanning the words and transmitting those symbols and letters to your RAS, which translates those images into thought patterns that allow you to understand what the images say. Developing that ability took you years, but now, it's automatic. It happens instantaneously for each letter and word that you are reading in a way that allows you to seamlessly flow from word to word, sentence to sentence without having to stop at each letter and go through the process. However, if this book were in a language you didn't know, your RAS would not be able to decipher its content because it has not been programmed to do so.

This example describes the process that takes place within your RAS to give meaning to one letter of one word on one page of one book. How many other things therefore are going on in your world every second? Your supercomputer is processing all this information for you and attempting to make sense of it as it stores it.

Let's go back to the concept of dropping a brick out a window. Our RAS has been programmed to accept the fact that the brick will fall without fail, but what would happen to our thinking if we went into space and dropped that same brick? It would float. Our RAS would then be programmed to provide us with another possibility and allow us to entertain another option of what might occur.

Life works the same way. Wherever you are in life right now, you are the sum of all your experiences. Your RAS has been accumulating data every second, and your computer has been programmed to evaluate billions of bits of data—experiences, sights, sounds, smells, feelings, tastes, and many others—and in so doing, you have made positive and negative associations. You've programmed your personal RAS to create meaning behind things. What might be a wonderful experience for one person might terrify another.

I mentioned my obsession with continuous improvement and the thousands of books I have read and continue to read voraciously, the thousands of hours of daily podcasts and audio programs I have listened to, the countless seminars I have attended, and the similarly minded friends and family I associate with. These things have fed and continue to feed my RAS, and I can use all this information. The outstanding things about our RAS is that it is always evolving.

I am confronted daily with a myriad of similar examples from my clients, including some who have been living with continuous physical and verbal abuse and countless other afflictions. For years, some have been told by their significant others things like these:

- You're unattractive.
- No one will ever want you if you leave me.
- No one will believe you.
- You deserve to be beaten.
- If you tell anyone, I'll kill you.
- If you leave, you'll end up destitute.
- If you leave, I'll fight you for custody of the children.

Imagine how you would react if someone close to you was going through this situation. From the outside looking in, it's easy to play armchair quarterback and simply say the individual must leave such a situation based on our conventional cultural beliefs in our RAS.

Unfortunately, however, the RAS of many victims of domestic abuse has been reprogrammed over time to conclude that these statements are true. They believe they're not good enough and deserve this type of treatment. Their abusers assert power and control over them in such a way and for such a period that their RAS has concluded these statements are true. Visualize for a moment these victims in the center of a circle around which their abusers are walking and with each step are attempting to reprogram their victims into believing all the above. Trailing behind them is a layer of cement. Each time they complete an additional revolution, they pour another layer of cement on the outer circle. Over time, each layer makes it more difficult for the victims to break through this circle of confinement. They feel helpless and paralyzed; they ultimately conclude that they deserve this treatment. They are isolated from the outside and are fearful about telling others; they don't have the strength and momentum to break through the cement. They're trapped.

Such victims who have made their way to me did so because they found a compelling reason to break through. I honor them for their courage. Their RAS had been changed; they thought they were deserving of the beatings, but when, say, their children started suffering abuse, that fueled them to reprogram their thinking and get help.

When they meet me in my office, I spend a lot of time developing trust, respect, and rapport. We engage in the breakdown phase, step one, of the Brutally Honest system in a wonderful journey to reconnecting themselves to their souls' cores, where they get back to their true, uncorrupted state of being and are alone with their thoughts. They are then able to develop their target zones, one of which is erasing the negative programming their abusers have instilled in them and reclaim their understanding of what a healthy relationship is, what they need to attain, and what they truly deserve.

If I find myself on the other side—representing abusers who inflict this type of pain on others—we engage in a similar process whereby they reach an understanding of their actions. They realize, acknowledge, and take accountability for their actions, and they begin reprogramming their RAS to associate negative associations with their actions.

Too many of these individuals—whether due to their upbringing or other factors—truly believe their actions are appropriate and that their victims deserve what they got. Their RAS justifies their actions based on its programming. I refer such individuals to professionals who are equipped to handle this reprogramming—anger-management specialists, counselors, psychologists, psychiatrists, and others. Each case is a unique situation that requires specialized, custom attention that addresses their unique factors.

Outside observers of the two different examples above reach immediate conclusions about what should be done, their feelings about the victims or abusers, and their beliefs about what they should do based on what their RAS have been programmed to believe. The advice I give these individuals is predictable; my RAS has been programmed differently than perhaps yours. It is the result of many years of representing thousands of similarly situated individuals, years of research, and seeing the results of that.

As I often say, the most powerful word in the English dictionary is *why*. Regardless of the issue or problem I am confronted with, I of course want to know how, what, when, and where something happened, but more than any of this, I systematically get to the why. This is very powerful. When you observe a weed appearing in a well-manicured lawn, the weed itself is the what. Below the surface is the actual source of the weed, its roots—the why. When I get to that level, I can begin making lasting change by reprogramming my or others' RAS to accept new possibilities, a new vision of their situations, and a clear, concise, compelling future with a myriad of positive possibilities.

Clients often present in any one of many psychological states due to recent occurrences or a long-standing history. These diagnoses and conditions are very real and disabling at times. Outsiders may say, "Get over it," or "Be strong," or "We all have our problems, so suck it up and move on." They believe the advice they are giving due to their RAS and upbringing. I put myself in their shoes so I can understand why they are acting the way they are or saying the things they are saying. Empathy, compassion, and a genuine fuel to want to help them allow me to begin getting them back on track to achieve their goals.

Part of this team process often finds me referring clients to trained counselors or other appropriate professionals. Seeking out such professionals is not something to be ashamed about. To the contrary, it takes great clarity, strength, and courage to want to make lasting changes. Through this combination of team members, we can begin to positively change our clients' RAS to evaluate and react to situations differently, to empower them, to uplift them, and to guide them and their children to a compelling future.

The main tool I use in my personal life and in my law practice to get to the whys is a journal. My most prized possession I will give to my children and grandchildren is my personal journal. It's where I capture all my thoughts and write what has gone well in my life and what has not. Most important, it's where I can see clearly why these things occurred. I go back from time to time to my journal to see how I handled a similar situation and the results. It's my guidebook for future generations on my beliefs, thoughts, and suggestions.

I have my law clients perform a similar exercise. They journal about the beginning of their relationships with their significant others and bring that to the present. Moving forward, they journal their daily events. I find that there is no better way to get inside their heads and learn why things occurred that brought them to me. It's cathartic for them, and it allows them to organize their thoughts and see why their RAS developed the way it has. By analyzing this, we can begin to develop their goals and start a journey toward them that will be guided and will avoid whatever in their past has caused them pain and utilize whatever has given them success and pleasure.

As you can see, RAS is an incredibly powerful tool we all have. Regardless of our situations, we all have the power to change and reprogram this part of our brain. Granted, some have biological or psychological impediments (mentioned above) that may make this process difficult or even impossible in severe cases. These individuals need appropriate professional treatment. Quite often in my practice, I refer clients to these professionals. No one going through a divorce, custody dispute, or other family law matters does so without some degree of emotional torment or depression; it's a difficult time. I frequently recommend professional intervention by way of counselors, psychologists, or in some cases medical doctors or psychiatrists. They perform a vital role in assisting clients through difficult times and are part of our clients' specifically tailored teams. These highly trained, competent professionals provide an elevated level of guidance that helps people reprogram their RAS.

So your powerful computer is being programmed twenty-four hours a day and is making associations between items it reviews and other items you tell it to match up with—cause and effect if you will. You programmed your RAS that to touch fire (cause) will produce pain (effect). You have at your disposal a system you can program to achieve great things much the same way you can program it to create devastation. Individuals such as Adolph Hitler convinced millions of his followers that Jews were bad and had to be exterminated. Their RAS truly believed that this was just and proper and had to be done. On the other hand, Mahatma Gandhi pioneered nonviolent resistance to tyranny, which led to India's independence and inspired movements for civil rights and freedom across the world. Both individuals created massive change to the belief systems (RAS) of the masses who followed them, both did so through vastly different methods, but both produced their desired results. We are living in a time when terror attacks occur almost daily. Terrorists are programmed to believe that by killing others by way of killing themselves in the process is a good thing that will give them eternal happiness.

With this background and newfound knowledge, you are now equipped to make the same massive change in your life and those of the people closest to you—your family, friends, coworkers, and anyone you meet. You are constantly feeding your RAS with content some of which is being controlled by others and some by you. TV and radio commercials and magazine ads directly and indirectly condition you to act, use, adopt, or purchase products or services. You need a defense mechanism that allows you to be aware of what's happening so you can make conscious decisions about how your RAS will be affected.

On the conscious side of things, you have immediate control of the positive programming of your RAS. The people you associate with, the places you visit, the books you read, how you spend your time, the television shows you watch, the seminars you attend, the schools you attend—there's an endless supply of potentially positive data you can use to fuel your RAS. This is the critical difference in beginning to recapture your life, refocus on where you are in life, developing your compelling future, being able to attack your current circumstances, and thrive in Generation Now.

Chapter 3

Confronting the Four-Letter Word

IN THE LAST CHAPTER, YOU LEARNED THAT YOUR THOUGHTS AND focus shape your life. You learned that there can be no obstacle overcome, goal achieved, or change made without your RAS being programmed to first seek it out and then achieve it. Like the body of an Olympic athlete that has been shaped by nutrient-rich foods, intense training, and unrivaled dedication, your brain must be fed daily with empowering thoughts, objectives, and focus. You cannot simply will something to happen, but when your will is combined with concentrated, intentional focus, the chances of reaching your target increase exponentially.

If it were that easy—simply concentrating, focusing, and mapping out a compelling future—why doesn't everyone simply do that? Why doesn't everyone obtain their goals? Great questions I have often asked myself. We all know people who can use our help, guidance, and assistance. We look at family, friends, and clients and pass judgment on them based on what we perceive; we cannot comprehend why some people act the way they do and fail to make changes in their lives that we know would make a difference.

The first part of this answer lies in our programmed perception. Whatever we perceive at this moment is the sum of the ingredients that went into creating our RAS. We all have belief systems of what is right and wrong. We think that if we did X, Y, and Z and the outcome was positive, everyone should simply do the same, right? We all judge others by our standards and the filters we have created over time, and we give what we consider genuine advice to others based on that to help them, but some people don't want advice, may not be ready to accept it, or simply don't want us involved.

I find myself in this situation often. I know in my heart I have information that can help others, and I find it difficult not to offer them advice when I know I can make a difference. But there's a difference between helping those seeking assistance and trying to help those who aren't looking for any help no matter how good our advice seems to us and how much we want to pass it on.

Those who come to me for legal advice are seeking my guidance and assistance, and I have helped many of them through difficult, tumultuous, and life-altering situations with my Brutally Honest system and have shown them how they can thrive, not just survive. As I mentioned, I have applied the Brutally Honest system in other situations—not just in legal settings—to help people evaluate their situations, plan, and ultimately achieve their goals. In this capacity, I have guided, mentored, and helped countless others who have sought my assistance. I revel in this position, and I take this responsibility very seriously. Because these individuals seek my assistance, they are most receptive to what I suggest. They acknowledge they need and want help, so they are in the best position to make radical, life-altering, positive change in their and their families' lives.

Others, however, are not as receptive to my assistance though I believe they need it and know it could make a difference. My RAS has conditioned me to seek out these individuals and help them, and I often find myself helping strangers or those I have just met. The reactions I get range from genuine appreciation to outright rejection. Whether it's a flaw or a genuine gift, it's nonetheless who I am. Weighing the choices of attempting to help versus ignoring the situation, I more often intervene, offer assistance, and take a chance on making a difference in someone's life. Unfortunately, despite my inherent mission to help, as I write this, some people very close to me refuse the suggestions I have for them, are dismissive of the thoughts, make jokes about them, or utilize many other defense mechanisms to avoid taking action. I feel personally responsible for failing to get through to them. What they also know is that I will never give up on them. How do you approach these situations? Do you make observations and lend assistance, or do you stay on the sidelines?

Whatever standards and values you have for yourself and family does not mean that these are the only options or that they are even correct; they are your values and standards period. At the same time as you are deciding whether to intervene and assist others, some have made a determination about you and are deciding whether they should reach out to you for help in overcoming a problem or attaining a result that they perceive to be a need in you. This endless cycle occurs every day. In my life, I revel in both positions. On the one hand, I believe I can make a difference in everyone's life, and I give advice accordingly. Likewise, I genuinely appreciate and seek out assistance and guidance from others who make a difference in my life. Whether it comes from a mentor, friend, client, family member, or one of the thousands of authors whose guidance I obtained, the assistance I have gotten and keep getting helps me daily. I learn from every interaction I have with anybody or anything I come in contact with, and I live according to the Japanese philosophy of *kaizen*— constant and never-ending improvement.

Those needing to change their lives and overcome their obstacles must first want to do so; they must have the will to want it. What is right for one may not be right for another or simply not something the other wants to do. Neither is right or wrong. If people want guidance or information, they must be receptive to it and its source. At that stage, their journeys can commence. As we learned, simply being at the starting line does not get us to the finish line; having the will to do this is the critical first step.

Once the journey begins, a paralyzing four-letter word can stop us in our tracks—*fear*. Before there is any chance of moving forward successfully toward a new, compelling future, people have to face their fears head-on. They have to visualize their fears, make them real— something they can see, taste, smell, feel, and hear. They have to be willing to dive off the board with the assurance that there is water below into which they will smoothly glide.

To help you create a process to overcoming fear, let's break that word down. Many will tell you that fear is False Evidence Appearing Real. I like that, and I have used it often. What is fear really? Let's take a different look one letter at a time. Perhaps after you read through the following, you will have a different perspective on fear:

Facing the truth
Elevating yourself above self-imposed barriers
Anticipating the path
Revving up your compelling future

Facing the Truth

Before you can attempt to break free of the chains holding you back, you must first face the truth as to how and why you are in your current place in life. I'm assuming that because you are reading this, you were adversely affected in one way or another by the tidal wave that hit our economy a couple of years back or simply want to make a change in some area of your life. At the time I am reviewing this—December 2017—the economy is hitting all-time highs, but you might be reading this during an economic slump. During the last recession, some of you incurred only minor damage while others were decimated.

Others are reading this to make other improvements in their lives, marriages, relationships with their children, or other areas unique to them. If you are one of the lucky ones who have not been adversely affected, I want to know what you did because you are among an incredibly small group of individuals. Even if you do exist, I imagine some people close to you have felt the wrath and could benefit by some of the suggestions in this book. I caution those who are living in times of abundance to not think they are economic wizards—what goes up must come down.

Facing the truth begins with taking personal accountability for your life. While there may have been many factors that contributed to your situation, only you have final accountability. No matter what may have occurred, you contributed in some way. Even if you had no control over the event that caused the problem, you absolutely did and have control over how you reacted to it and what you did about it. I am not downplaying the many other reasons that may have contributed to the issue. Greedy bankers, lying Wall Street executives, rampant cheating and stealing, big banks threatening closing while others closed, mortgage defaults, greedy consumers who got in over their head with real estate, the decline of the stock market, pensions eroding, 401(k)s being cut in half, student loans—all caused the economic implosion. As I write this in February 2018, after many years of an incredible bull market, in the week ending February 9, 2018, the market sunk quicker than at any time in history losing more than 12 percent in a matter of days with 1,000-plus-point swings to close the week at 24,190. Here we go again. Panic? No. You will learn why these things are fairly predictable over the history of the market.

In my law practice, I have the pleasure of meeting and assisting countless individuals going through a myriad of horrible circumstances—spouses who threaten to kill them if they tell anyone they are being abused, threats of financial power, threats to take the children, threats to tell their families about closely guarded secrets, fears of how they will survive without any education, and many other threats. These are again all very real and serious situations. I tell my clients it's a lot easier giving advice sitting on the other end the desk as opposed to living their lives. Here is where empathy, compassion, and sensitivity come in.

You may be confronted with a serious medical condition—yours or a loved one's—having to care for elderly parents, worry associated with simply being a parent, sibling, daughter, or son, or many of the day-to-day challenges with running a family or household. Have you lost a job, been demoted, or had to move across the country to keep your job? Are you unable to pay your student loans? Forced to drop out of college because you couldn't afford it? Were you promised something by someone who didn't come through?

These things are real. Many were not initially caused by you directly, and many you had no control over directly, but they are all terrible. Many families have had their lives turned upside down overnight. That pit in your stomach is real. Retirees forced to go back to work or delay retirement, record foreclosures forcing individuals out of their homes, and so on. Families destroyed by the breakdown of the family unit, divorce causing one household to become two with two sets of rules and expectations. Where there may have been an agreement early in the happy marriage that one spouse gives up a career to raise the children as a stay-at-home parent while the other spouse works to support the household, all rules change in a divorce. Individual lives are radically changed. A spouse who has been out of the workforce for years is forced to confront the world in a whole new way with fear of the unknown. Having dealt with thousands of these situations, I assure my clients that they will be okay and must see life through a new filter with new tools to get them through the instant fear and focus on taking the necessary steps to create a compelling future one step at a time.

When you receive a blow of monumental proportions, it is easy and normal to want to blame others or feel sorry for yourself. In 2005, after going from lifting weights, training in and teaching martial arts, being in peak physical condition, running a successful law firm, and having an outstanding family, I went to having a tumor on my spinal cord that radically changed my world in a month. I went from doing jump-spinning sidekicks and lifting hundreds of pounds of weight to being paralyzed.

Four surgeries later and after four months of recovery followed by lasting impediments, my life was radically transformed. At one time, I did not want to be positive, did not want to listen to positive audios, read positive books, and so on. I simply lay on a recovery bed in my living room watching TV and listening to sports radio day and night. I buried my head in the sand thinking it would all go away. Chapter 10 of *The Brutally Honest Life Management Journal* comes from my personal journal; it chronicles this experience for a year—from when my symptoms started all the way to recovery. It shows all my emotions then, and it shows what got me through it—how and why.

As I sit here thirteen years later in 2018, I still have figurative and real scars from those days. I have learned to create a new norm. While I may be lifting weights differently, do cardio differently day, and my weight may be less, I have new issues such as the loss of left-arm strength from another benign tumor, a red blood count decline causing extreme energy loss, kidney failure last year, appointments with every doctor with an "ist" at the end of his or her name, and many other obstacles, but they were just that—obstacles. My life is my life. No matter what life has thrown at me, I simply considered it me and my norm. I am beyond blessed for everything the good Lord has given me and for all I have achieved. I don't whine or complain. I wake up and stick to habits and routines that work for me and my family. Regardless of the difficulty or pain, I adjust my workouts and fight through them. With each new obstacle, I simply reach into my toolbox and face it as I have in the past with the tools that got me through previously—tenacity, courage, passion, commitment, focus, and drive. I have no idea what the Lord has in store for me, but I trust he has a plan. What I can do, however, is remain positive, live life to the fullest, help as many others as I can, and be thankful every day.

Facing the truth necessitates putting everything in perspective and no matter what, be at the top of the accountability list. Many will take issue with that; those who know me know I wear my heart on my sleeve. I am brutally honest. I have shared my personal journey to help others see but one way to overcome and confront obstacles. I also relayed this so as not to appear hypocritical. I went through many of the thoughts and emotions you may be going through, and I go through them every day. I understand, however, that this is normal. The difference is what we do each day notwithstanding our thoughts and feelings.

In addition to the physical side of things, I and the rest of the world went through the ups and downs and even more downs of the stock market years back only to come back soaring. I saw my net worth take a ride on the world's most crazy, winding, twisting roller coaster in swings that previously occurred over a year, not in a day.

Fortunately, I stuck to the very core of the Brutally Honest belief system, the journal. I kept almost daily through my physical transformation in 2005 and my recovery in 2006, through the ups and downs that life threw my way all the way through the past economic tsunami and all the way to the latest recovery. I recorded how bad I felt at times, what I had done wrong, what I should have done differently, and so on. That caused me to take personal accountability for what went wrong and allowed me to focus on what had happened and why. It allowed me to take inventory of what the cause really was.

Even if I did not find all the reasons, I had a working template to make sense of it. It allowed me also to realize who was in my inner circle, the people who gave me their unconditional love and support. It also brought to the surface those were weren't that way. I began to put together my bull's-eye theory with those closest to me in the bull's-eye itself. As the rings go out from there, the degree of unconditional support slowly ebbs. You can visibly see who will be there as life throws you its inevitable hurdles. You also see who is in the outer rings. Some you socialize with, work with, attend seminars with, and so on; their roles are limited to these events. This information and knowledge is priceless! By taking account of your resources, you will be able to go forth empowered and better positioned to overcome the next set of similar obstacles.

If your marriage is not at its best, why is that? Is it because you married someone who turned out to be the opposite of what you thought? Have drugs or alcohol played a part? If so, have you sought help? Has anger or rage been a central part? If so, has anger management taken place? Have economic forces taken over such as losing money, losing a job, or bad financial decisions? Have your children caused problems? Have they been disrespectful, angry, addicted to drugs or alcohol, or in trouble at school or with the law? Have you simply grown apart based on differences of opinions and values? What part of the causes are you responsible for? Are there things you can simply or not so simply change but you have not done so simply due to pride or wanting to hold your ground? Can marriage counseling solve your problems or at least give you an opportunity to do so? Quite simply, there are ways to salvage most marriages if steps are taken early on to make changes. Step one, however, is wanting to change, and that's followed closely by step two—taking accountability and responsibility for your part of your problems.

A true win-win is where both sides come to the table and get 80 percent of what they want by being willing to concede 20 percent to come to an agreement that works for both. Where one side insists on 100 percent, that's a dictatorship, and that never works. Many cases I deal with go through many of the steps mentioned above. They try empathy, try communicating their displeasure, may use spiritual intervention or religious counseling, and may try therapy, counseling, and sometimes, they see the end in sight. But even in those cases, I still explore whether there are any stones left unturned. I attempt to see if any form of individual or couples therapy could help.

As a family law attorney, I believe in the sanctity of the family and as such explore all ways to attempt to salvage a marriage before moving forward with a divorce or custody agreement. In so doing, I ask my clients poignant and direct questions to find out what their parts in their breakdowns were. Just as a medical doctor would, I diagnose my patients and prescribe ways for them to get through their tough times.

If you lost money in the stock market, why? Did you simply let your money stand stagnant? Could you have reallocated yearly to have been better diversified? Could you have sold? Did you have too much in one stock? Should you have moved money to a cash position? Were you day-trading attempting to make a lot of money quickly instead of being a long-term investor? Were you managing your portfolio as opposed to having a professional do that? Did you bury your head in the sand and not get out when you could have? Were you on the sidelines, not in the market?

Did you lose your job? Why? While it's possible that was due to random downsizing, unless the company went out of business, there existed the possibility that you were let go based on your perceived lack of value to the company. Did you have the best work ethic possible? Did you perform above and beyond for personal pride and not because you were seeking praise? Did you approach work with a sense of entitlement to raises and bonuses simply because you were working there? What could you have done differently? Did your negative attitude toward your fellow team members cause problems?

Did you stop when things got easy and just coasted, or did you try to improve your performance? People with personal pride and a great work ethic always improve and raise their game and skills. I guarantee you that they will be less likely to be downsized than those who simply show up to work. They likewise will be rewarded for going above and beyond.

Did you lose your home? Why? Was it because of random life events or due at least in part to something you did or perhaps didn't do? Did you take a home equity loan to redo the kitchen for the fourth time or to take exotic vacations?

Were you forced to postpone retirement? Why? Was it due to your employer, or was it due in part to your choices of what you invested in, how you invested, or whether you invested in your retirement fund? Perhaps you did not do your own due diligence each year to gain the knowledge about the various funds you were invested in. What was your net worth five years ago compared to today? Is it going in the right direction? Why or why not?

Taking personal accountability means not making excuses for the results and/or our reactions to our circumstances. As painful as this may be to do, as painful as it is to acknowledge that we may have done things differently, it is a critical first step in facing our fears, creating plans, and moving forward to ensure we don't repeat the same mistakes.

Likewise, when evaluating your life, it's critically important to focus on what has gone well. What great things are going on in your life now? What positive resources do you have that you can utilize to assist the other areas of your life that need improvement? While your finances may have taken a hit, your family may be solid and strong. Contrarily, many of my clients come to me with marriage and family problems while their networks of friends, their careers, their faith, their health, or any combination of infinite possibilities are going very well. When you are going through a crisis or a difficult period, it's not easy to see and appreciate what's going right in your life; many tend to focus only on what's wrong. As you start making changes to those areas of your life, don't lose sight of the many blessings you have that you should be thankful for.

Elevating Yourself above Self-Imposed Barriers

You have begun to focus on what you believe the reason is for the negative outcomes in your life, how you felt about them, and how they affected you and the people you love. You determined you needed to take accountability for your contributions to the situation and many other contributing factors. You have made a mental inventory of these things to make some sense of why you are where you are.

When something painful happens to us, our internal defense mechanisms search for ways to make us feel better about our situation. Blaming others—spouses, children, significant others, the economy, politicians, bankers, mortgage companies, and countless other people, places, and things—makes us feel a little better than if we blame ourselves. See whether any of the following sounds familiar:

- If only my spouse and kids would have stopped nagging me, I wouldn't have to drink, do drugs, or get angry.
- If only the government warned us sooner or did its job better.
- If only that mortgage broker had told me I couldn't really afford that new home.
- If only the management of the company I bought stock in did their jobs, it wouldn't have dropped in value.
- My broker should have told me to go to cash.
- My old employer is responsible for my current economic problems for letting me go. How dare them! After all, I showed up at work each day and did my job.
- How can God (or fill in any other higher being you may believe in) do this to me? It's not fair.

Blaming others tends to make us feel better about ourselves. "It wasn't my fault," we say, but does that really help? No. No matter what you tell yourself about the reason for the situation good, bad, or indifferent, the reality will always be that the problem existed—it happened, and the effects have been problematic. If we can't agree on that, let's agree on something else. If we continue doing what we have done in the past, we'll likely get the same results. If we don't make changes with the future in mind, we'll likely be in the same place in the future.

How do we start breaking through our self-imposed barriers? We have already taken step one above—we listed our beliefs as to how things occurred in our lives. We know that to make a breakthrough, we must take personal responsibility for our lives.

Part of the reason we blame others is that we tell ourselves we didn't have the ability to have predicted or avoided the situations. This faulty reasoning is due to our creating self-imposed barriers that pacify us by telling us that there is a reason we cannot do something. It creates an excuse that convinces us we cannot impact our destinies. Someone else is in control; we're just along for the ride. These are only a few of the barriers we place on ourselves.

These negative associations are being programmed in our RAS and accepted as truth. It's like the way abusers of drugs displace reality with drugs and become accustomed to avoiding their problems that way. While under the effects of the drug, they believe the underlying problem is gone. But as the drug wears off, they realize the problem is still there and in most cases worse. The solution? Take more drugs to avoid the problems. However, that can lead to serious addiction and/or death.

If we are to stand a chance of changing our current situation, we need to change our thinking. We need to tell ourselves that we can do things we used to say we couldn't. We need to find answers we once thought never even existed. We need to leave open the possibility that there is a solution and a compelling future beyond the wall that stands in our minds' way. We need to see ourselves smashing through that wall.

Look at the list we wrote earlier again with this new twist:

- I am so thankful and blessed to have a spouse and children to share this great world with and to be there for and with me unconditionally. I am thankful we all feel secure enough with each other to express our feelings.
- Thankfully, I obtained enough information from many sources to make fully informed decisions about what various governmental agencies were telling me.
- I am so glad that I stuck to my budget and utilized the help of others (accountants, financial advisers, etc.) to talk me out of buying a home I knew I couldn't afford.
- Thankfully I was well diversified, and though I lost money, it wasn't as bad as those who hadn't diversified.
- I did my homework about my stocks with my broker's help, which kept me out of troubled stocks.
- I have my job today because I have an outstanding work ethic. I exceed the goals and expectations my boss has of me because I

always go above and beyond. I live by my high standards, and my employer recognizes that. I wasn't laid off because of that.

- Thank you, Lord for all my blessings and the wonderful things in my life.

What could you have done differently to avoid the reasons for your economic woes? What self-imposed barriers do you have that may be holding you back? How do these barriers affect your thinking and the way you conduct your life? What can you do today to destroy or change your self-imposed barriers? How will doing that positively affect your life?

As I stated early on, this is not a get-rich-quick process; it won't make a bad marriage good overnight or prompt your disrespectful children to suddenly start respecting you.

Take the economy for example. Most Americans' thinking was plain wrong when they told themselves the economy was doing so well based on our knowledge and skill. That reasoning led many Americans to take risks because almost everything they did was working. Stocks will double in value in a month. Real estate values are going through the roof. Jobs are plentiful. The economy's thriving. When these things are going well, the divorce rate is steady or decreases because many of the contributing factors to divorce—finances, frustration, uncertainty, and unemployment among them—are stable. With this thinking, many think, *Why not double and triple the risk the next time?* They became accustomed to instantaneous increases in their net worth. Of course, it was due to their stellar knowledge, right?

By replacing this faulty thinking with reasonable thinking, we can break down the barriers between us and our compelling, rewarding futures. Envision these barriers as walls we can't see through or over. By a change in perception and reality, we begin to initially chip through these walls, gain momentum, start pounding on them with a sledgehammer, and then plow through them with a bulldozer. Once the walls have been destroyed, we'll see a new path ahead and begin to forge our compelling futures filled with abundance.

Anticipating the Path

Once you have assessed your past and have taken inventory of why you are in your current situation good or bad, it's time to create a compelling vision of your the future and a path to get there one brick at a time instead of getting caught up in the immediate gratification mentality. Those with that mentality forget conventional wisdom and the tried-and-true rules, decide they have expertise they don't, rely on so-called experts with little or no expertise, and indulge in self-centered, egotistical, and self-destructive ways.

Social networking has proven to be a dynamic enhancement to our lives. As I write this, Facebook is the billion-dollar behemoth that has become part of our culture. Consider Facebook, My Space before that, LinkedIn, Twitter, and countless other forms of social media such as Snapchat and Instagram; whatever your thoughts are of them, they have transformed the way we interact with others. It has also been the main source of communication of President Trump. While the message is often debated, the fact that a president uses this technology is amazing. Before these forms of social networking there was (and still is) conventional email. If you want to see just how fast this new, technological age has changed, simply read this sentence where I refer to email as almost extinct. I would really be dating myself if I referred to the stone ages when people actually wrote handwritten letters and mailed them off.

Social networking allows people to catch up with others all over the globe in an instant. People we may not have seen in decades are now back in our lives with a simple click. I find this useful; I enjoy connecting with friends, client's old and new. Despite privacy and "big brother" issues, social media is here to stay.

I run contrary to all the legal advisers by utilizing social networking in my law practice. Interacting with my clients on this level allows me to get to know them and their families, friends, and environments, which allows me to represent them fully. As their legal advocate, I am their voice; it's up to me to tell their stories to the court and the world if necessary. Judges who enter courtrooms for new cases know little about the facts of the case. It is up to me as my clients' representative to give life, passion, energy, and perspective to their stories. It's my job to bring a case number to life.

Through many meetings with the client, their journals, and social media, I transcend the pages of documents and bring each of their diverse stories to life. Likewise, social media allows my clients to interact with me in a personal environment away from the courtroom and legal environment and see the person behind the Armani suits. When I step foot into a courtroom, I wear the required uniform of the trade. As a representative of my client, I am at times the first visual representation of the client's case a judge sees. It amazes me at the way some attorneys dress when they appear in this role for clients. Your appearance in court is a subliminal sign of your respect for the judge, the court, and the time-honored system itself. I appear in court in custom Italian suits, monogrammed fitted shirts, a pair of one of my hundreds of theme based cufflinks, distinctive shoes, and one of my many different automatic watches; I consider these the tools of my trade that show my respect for the court. I take pride in myself and let my clients know I believe in them and their cases. It also allows me to combine an infinite arrangement of looks to best demonstrate what I am trying to achieve on that day.

That said, however, beneath my exterior, I'm my true self. I prefer to be at home with my family or in our mountain home in a pair of sweats simply hanging out with Monica and the kids playing games, watching movies, writing, playing with our two Doberman's and a myriad of other laid-back activities. Through Facebook and other social media, my friends see me in that capacity. The ability to interact with clients as simply Greg helps me to genuinely and fully engage with them. It also allows me to ensure that my clients aren't saying or posting anything on their public profiles that could be used against them in their legal cases.

This has transformed into an untapped minefield for family law litigators when representing their clients. Some people appear in court as if they were the mothers or the fathers of the year while they post pictures of themselves on Facebook doing Jell-O shots off others' stomachs. When I began practicing law, we used (and still do) private investigators to follow individuals to see if they could get photos or other evidence to use in court. Today, within minutes, online, individuals voluntarily offer this information up. Facebook and others like it allow individuals to interact behind a keyboard often in anonymity or even when known in a fearless environment. It's much easier to say something online in the privacy of your living room than it may be to do so at a social setting, bar, restaurant, or somewhere else where you are face to face.

This environment of safety has also caused a significant spike in online and other extramarital affairs. Before the internet and social networking, those who felt upset, disconnected, or underappreciated by spouses or significant others would find conventional way to address the issue such as communicating with them, counseling, or simply time. Today, those who feel slighted are confronted with old friends, boyfriends, or girlfriends who become friends online and tell them how good they look, how much they miss them, and so on. These individuals, who may already be vulnerable and have low self-esteem, develop allies and begin to open up to these newfound friends. One thing leads to another, and in many cases, these otherwise benign comments that start as attempts to help lead to inappropriate acts, including affairs. In my practice, social networking has morphed beyond belief to where it is involved to some degree in most of my cases.

So should we use social media or not? To each his own, but discretion online is a necessity as it is in any social occasion. Caution and common sense will allow you to gain all of social media's benefits while avoiding its pitfalls.

We must keep in mind that we are the ultimate gatekeepers of what we do, what advice we take, whom we listen to, what technology we embrace, what we say and do online, how much, and when and where— not the experts, your broker, lawyer, agent, neighbor, relatives, friends, or anyone else. We alone are our ultimate decision makers.

As mentioned in the introduction, Brutally Honest comprises three steps that make it different from conventional self-help programs. In step one, the breakdown phase, we go backward before we go forward toward our goals. We descend to the magical place called our soul's core and shed all stereotypes. We get rid of what our brother, sister, aunt, uncle, neighbor, television gurus, or leaders are suggesting and find ourselves alone with ourselves, our decisions, and our thoughts. To do otherwise would mean we would be making these monumental, life-changing decisions based on what everyone else wants, not us. It is here and only here that we say we are ready to develop compelling futures in step two followed by beginning the journey in step three.

In the first two steps above (letters *F* and *E* of the word *fear*), you in fact arrived at that place assuming you were brutally honest with yourself. By being personally accountable for your current place in this world, you have taken the critical step of being honest with yourself. Now and only now can you truly develop your path to your compelling future.

At this point, we want to do whatever will increase our chances of success and decrease our chances of taking on additional problems. In a perfect world, we'd simply envision a straight line toward our goals, but things don't always work out the way we want or expect them to. The recent wild rides the economy has taken taught us that for sure and has given us newfound respect for conventional thought.

As you build your path forward, you will use whatever has worked well for you to push you toward your goals and avoid what you had found to be problematic or painful. You will also use the past to help you predict and anticipate hurdles in your way forward. By envisioning these problems, you will no doubt eliminate many of them from even occurring. Is that overly simple? Yes, but what you should be asking is why it's simple. During past upswings in the economy when everything you did worked, you had no reason to engage in such futuristic analysis. Logic and analysis went out the window. But in Generation Now, after learning that this reasoning was flawed, you realize you must plan, analyze, focus, and use the tools that will give you the best chance of success and keep you from repeating mistakes. This will not guarantee success, but it will increase the odds in your favor.

This is the time for some clarification. What does the phrase *becoming wealthy* mean to you? Most people think of wealth in terms of money, but I respectfully suggest another possibility. Wealth can mean many things other than money. For me, wealth has many different levels. Think of wealth as a bull's-eye. At the center of it, my definition of wealth is the love and respect of my family. The next ring includes my health, my closest friends, and so on. Don't get me wrong; money is a necessary requirement for life, but if you have money at the center of your world, ask yourself why. There's confusion surrounding the biblical passage that people think reads, "Money is the root of all evil," but the passage actually reads, "The *love* of money is the root of all evil." Money is but a tool that allows us to be wealthy with wealth being the infinite ways you can define it.

There's great controversy in the world about those with money compared to those who don't have it—the so-called 1 percent versus the 99 percent. I won't debate the matter in this book as that is not its purpose, but the underlying message is that correctly used, money can make a world of positive difference, but if used improperly, it can destroy lives.

In my profession as a family law attorney, I see every day the horror stories caused by such faulty thinking. I have seen countless individuals seemingly having it all—lots of money, wonderful spouses and families, big homes, and huge net worth's, but due to too many reasons to list, they decided that wasn't enough and made poor decisions that caused their whole proverbial houses to come crumbling down. They gave in to greed, temptation, momentary weakness, perceived boredom, or a desire for excitement without taking time to see what was right in front of them. Almost overnight, they ended up depressed and poor while their innocent spouses and families were forced to pick up the pieces and move on.

What I have also found is that what appears on the surface is not always the whole story. I spend a great deal of time speaking with my clients because I want to get well below the surface while not wanting to cast legal, moral, social, or ethical judgment. I want to find out what had caused them to step over the line or act the way they did. I have represented faulty and innocent spouses alike and have learned that when I look far enough, I'll find culpability in both individuals. Let me be perfectly clear—I'm certainly not implying that a victim of abuse deserves to be abused or a spouse deserves to be cheated on. Absolutely not. What I do know is that when you look deep enough, you can find a triggering event that caused faulty spouses to act as they did. It could be an abusive upbringing, a lack of love growing up, the lack of a family unit, faulty belief systems, cultural differences, religious views, and many other things. Certain religions and cultures have radically different views on husbands' and wives' roles. I also see great degrees of psychological impediments and addictions that lead to these problems. Likewise and often, it really is simple stupidity.

To anticipate the path you have ahead of you and develop your compelling future, you first have to have a clear vision of what your ideal future looks like. For the purposes of defining this using the Brutally Honest system, we look ten years into the future as the point to develop your Brutally Honest Target Zones; we assume you'll be alive and thriving ten years from now at the very least. Only time will tell what will actually happen, but it's easier to hit a stationary target. Take a few minutes and visualize what your ideal life will look like in ten years:

- Where are you living?
- With whom?
- How's your health?
- Are you exercising? How?
- Are you working? Where?
- What is your title/job duties?
- Are you retired? Where?
- What's your net worth?
- What does it consist of? Investments? Savings? Real estate? Businesses? Retirement plans? Other?
- Are you married?
- How long?
- What is your relationship like?
- Do you have children and/or grandchildren? How many?
- What is your relationship with them like?
- What are your hobbies?
- What are your passions?
- Who are your friends?
- Who's your best friend?
- What impact have you had on the world?
- Was it good? Bad? Why?

These are but a few of the endless things you can visualize. Remember—it's your visualization, so have fun with it and be creative, open, and honest. Paint a very visible picture in your mind. See it, colorize it, taste it, smell it. Be it! Journal a concise summary of your most idealistic life ten years from now, and then add a paragraph about why you feel you must achieve this vision. There is a big difference when you program your RAS to hope or wish something will happen compared to making it an absolute must. How will your life and that of your family be different when you achieve this vision?

As you move forward toward your vision, it is possible but not probable you will achieve it by yourself. With each additional member, mentor, adviser, and resource you add, your odds of success increase tremendously. This assumes, however, that these resources are positive and beneficial and add value to your quest. You are as good as those you surround yourself with.

In my law practice, I find it heart-wrenching to see the most wonderful, beautiful, and well-intentioned clients telling me example after example of betrayal, emotional abuse, physical abuse, and systematic attacks on their self-esteem. I meet wonderful, beautiful people who believe they are ugly, terrible individuals because that's how someone has programmed their RAS. What they internalize from abusive people in their lives becomes self-fulfilling prophecies.

I'm very encouraged when clients tell me their most sacred and deep-seated feelings and emotions; that gives me the opportunity to make a difference in their and their children's lives. I can help them stop their self-destructive beliefs, get them the proper counseling or therapy if needed, develop a legal plan to stop the underlying problems, and help them develop new, compelling visions for the future. I help them gain self-empowering beliefs with the help of a support system comprising a legal team that will fight for them and their families and friends that will keep them on track.

I encourage my clients to surround themselves with people who genuinely want them to get to their next level of success and happiness. There is no better feeling than that of giving and receiving pure, absolute, and unconditional love. It is a heartfelt wish for others' happiness regardless of their flaws, mistakes, or imperfections. How many people in your life fit this definition? Do you give some people unconditional love or secretly wish they never surpass you? The first step is simply doing the exercise you just did. Consciously asking these challenging questions will result in your obtaining honest answers.

Seeking out mentors and others who support your values, morals, and goals will put you in a much better position for successfully obtaining your target zones. When seeking out mentors, be ultra-respectful of their time and efforts they are giving you. You should do your best to add value to them as well and pass on what you learn to others. By teaching others, you will continue to learn, grow, and reinforce old rules you may have forgotten. Anticipating the path will allow you to focus on where you want to end up and that will greatly increase your chances of success.

Revving Up Your Compelling Future

Now that you have assessed your past, analyzed your present, and began to define your path forward, it's time to start down that path. You are different from the majority who will continue to live their lives paralyzed by fear and wondering what's in the future and what's in their paths. You have developed a clear, compelling picture of where you want to go, and you started to put the pieces together to develop your path. You create it after evaluating many people, places, and things that can help you get there and not letting others tell you where you should be, whom you should listen to, and where you should be headed.

Many wonderful books have been written about success, time management, investments, religion, family, marriage, business success, and countless other topics, and I'll add this shameless plug for *The Brutally Honest Life Management Journal*, which provides a comprehensive look at all areas of your life to assist you in creating a compelling future. Where that book provides a detailed analysis of people's pasts, assesses their futures, and creates a vision and plan for the future, this book attacks Generation Now by confronting all the obstacles that cause us to create a view different from what we have been conditioned to believe. Depending on what areas of our lives we want to work on, we should seek out books and partake in other resources such as coaching, seminars, and the like.

Those who tend to stay paralyzed in fear tend to believe they are the only ones who can solve their problems; they have always relied on themselves to get them where they are. That may have helped them achieve what they have, and they think, *If it's not broke, don't change it.* And when things are going well for them, they think they have no reason to change. They mistakenly assume they are the sole reason for their success and thus blindly continue doing the same things and expecting the same results. They think they have the secret to success, but they aren't equipped to deal with the radical changes life can throw at them. Even though they can achieve success, it's often not for the reasons they think, and they cannot see beyond the present to what is coming in Generation Now.

Others are not happy with their lives or what they have achieved thus far. Others had left doors open for them, so they've gotten used to simply walking through them. But once they find those doors closed, they freeze up in fear not knowing why it's closed or how to open it.

In my law practice, I represent both types of individuals. In the first category are people who seem successful in many areas of life, but not far below the surface, they are unhappy in their marriages or relationships with their significant others, and their children may be suffering. Below the surface are hurts, worries, and fears. They're used to getting their way, having all the answers, and cruising through life. They achieved what they have by following patterns that yielded great results. But when they're faced with economic downturns, losses of jobs, addictions, and countless other variables, these same amazing, well-intentioned people find themselves not equipped to deal with such changes, and as a result, their relationships tend to suffer either through their actions that changed, their spouses or significant others changing, their children changing, or a combination of these.

I represent many powerful type A personalities, CEOs, professional athletes, entrepreneurs, and others who appear to have it all until they sit across from me and come to tears because they have no idea how their relationships had turned around so quickly. Some resort to anger, violence, sex, drugs, alcohol, or other temporary fixes to their problems that over time destroy them and their families. Some do not resort to these temporary fixes, but their relationships are affected because their spouses weren't equipped to handle the drastic changes affecting them. It is difficult and sad to see clients becoming emotional wrecks because they want to salvage their marriages but their spouses do not. Relationships change for a very wide variety of reasons. Some have the ability to change as their situations do but lack the clarity, understanding, or knowledge of the right tools to guide them through their roadblocks.

On the other side of the coin are clients who are spouses of type A personalities. They may have been long-term, supportive spouses who stayed home to raise the children and manage their households while their spouses rose the ladder of success in their careers. In such cases, these people who were used to success at home and with their children are confronted with radical changes based on one or more of the previously discussed dynamics. As this wave overcomes their families and causes their relationships to erode, they or their spouses are not equipped to get through these troubling times. These people are particularly near and dear to my heart in that they are in desperate need of help and are paralyzed with economic and emotional fears and desperately need answers.

In both of the above scenarios, people have been accustomed to doing the same things day in and day out and achieving predictable results. They both were able to get through the same door each day whether it was always open or if they had earned the key to open it. They then find it has become a steel door with new locks, and they have no idea what to do next. Their minds start wandering, and they begin devastating, destructive self-talk with themselves:

- Where will I get money for myself and children to live on?
- Where will I live?
- How will I feed my children?
- I'll never find anyone to love me again.
- I don't have any job skills.
- I can't support my family.

- I destroyed my children.
- Maybe my spouse was right and this is all my fault.
- I'm a bad person.

Whatever reason brings them to my office, I am always grateful for the opportunity to help them identify what's really going on. I refer them to other professionals who can assist them, we develop a plan to create solutions to their problems, and I assure them we will be there for them and empower them. By comforting them, reviewing their journals, and providing guidance and resources to alleviate their fears, we help them look at the new door in their paths and find keys to unlock it. We help them walk through the door and see their bright, compelling futures waiting for them and their children. I've seen tears of fear turn into tears of joy.

As we confront Generation Now, we too will find many locked doors and scramble through our key rings searching for the one that used to open doors. Simply recognizing that we are in a new world with new obstacles as well as new, wonderful possibilities will be the first step to navigating these new times. By recognizing that times are different, finding new resources, being willing to think and act differently, and seeing the world as such, we will be empowered with the tools and keys necessary to rev up first to survive and then to sur-thrive. Welcome to Generation Now.

Chapter 4

The Survival Course

OKAY, YOU'RE ONBOARD AND UNDERSTAND THAT YOU'RE LIVING IN A radically different time, that the old ways of doing things do not guarantee the same results, and that you need a new focus, a new level of understanding, and new resources to unlock the many doors in front of you.

Once you've recognized the above and are willing to move forward with this newfound understanding, your life will begin to change for the better. You will have fun as you learn, grow, and accumulate new keys. You will feel truly empowered as you open new door after new door in your path toward your compelling future.

It is extremely satisfying to see people I had seen in a state of fear transcend into empowered enlightenment as they see how bright the world truly is with its infinite potential. As they see, taste, feel, smell, and touch their new, compelling future, they often for the first time in a long time recapture that special part of themselves that may have been lost, suspended, or beaten down. They take back their and their children's lives, recognize things are different, and have splendors and possibilities to discover.

As I review this chapter in the fall of 2017, I look out the window of my home office on a wet, rainy, dreary day—overcast, gloomy, and dark. Lady and Ruby are sleeping on the rug in front of me. I write this in our home we have been in for a few years. My mind wanders back to when I started writing this book a few years earlier. I wrote the following in my home office of our previous home. Read the difference perspective can bring:

> As I sit staring out the window on a cold, blustery winter
> day, I gaze out my window of my home office to see the

most unbelievably beautiful newly fallen white snow that covers all the trees, shrubbery and my backyard. Words cannot describe how beautiful this view is. When I last was in this same seat the night before, the shade was closed, the backyard was black, dry and appeared ominous as nightfall cast its darkness over the yard lending a sense of unknown as to what was out in the dark world. Just twelve hours later, that same landscape now provides peace and serenity and amazing beauty. If I was unwilling or did not know how to open the shade of my office window, I would not even know what was on the side of the thin pane of glass.

Once I saw that however, all the wonderful sensations began to transform my prior beliefs of the darkened scene. I can now see the difference. I then got up, an accompanied by Lady and Ruby, my two loving, dedicated, loyal and playful Doberman Pinscher's, we unlocked the back door, and like two twin turbos (Their nick names by the way), they sprinted into the fresh white snow enjoying their new playground. As I walked out behind them I literally stopped in my tracks taking time to be thankful for this beautiful gift, for my family, friends, and clients and for all the great things that I have in my life right now. All my other senses ignited as I not only saw the beauty, I could smell the winter wonderland, touch the snow, taste the snowflakes as they landed on my face and in my mouth and hear, or not hear, the trees gently adjusting with the extra weight of the snow accumulating. You see, if I wanted to, I could focus on the pains in my body from yesterday's workout, problems from my past, whether I am hungry, world problems, or a million other things that would create negative feelings in my RAS. I CHOSE however to focus on this amazing scene and all the things that are going "right" in my life and not what is going "wrong." Does this make the problems go away? Of course not. What it does do is nourishes my mind with the best positive nutrition I can muster to put me in a better state, to be able to deal with and confront any hurdles in my path.

With this attitude of gratitude, I am much better equipped with new keys to unlock the doors in my path.

Fast-forward to the day I am typing this very line in January 2018 as I do another review of the book. I am in our current home, the one I wrote about above as I looked out on a gloomy fall day. Last night, several inches of beautiful white snow fell. This morning, despite a different home, a larger yard, once again, Lady and Ruby ran full out without a concern in the world. They run full speed navigating walls, rocks, trees, and slippery snow without hesitation and with an amazing sense of fun freedom. They could have walked outside, felt the cold snow, and turned around. They weren't worried about the economy, work, food, natural disasters, jobs, or other concerns; they simply played without reservation. They did so while being fully focused on catching one of the rabbits that come in each night to their yard.

While our lives cannot be compared to that of dogs, it does give us something to think about insofar as living life to the fullest, having fun in the process, being thankful for what we have, and making the best of our environment regardless of how the landscape changes from day to day. Life is what we make of it.

What will you make of the rest of your life as you begin Generation Now? Let's find out.

SECTION 2

MOVING FROM SURVIVING TO THRIVING

Chapter 5

Twenty-Five to Thrive

NOW WHAT? WE SPENT THE FIRST PART OF THE BOOK ANALYZING A myriad of reasons why we have run into problems with the economy and life, and we looked at those problems' possible causes. We all can play armchair quarterback and speculate as to what causes something to occur, and while there are many passionate individuals who profess to have the answers, the reality is that there are an infinite number of ingredients and combinations that may have all played a part in the outcome.

As we develop and evolve over the years, we become the sum of our experiences up to that point. What we say and do reflect our beliefs, which are constantly changing. Some is skill, some is based on conscious learning, and others are based on random luck and timing. As such, while we can spend countless hours watching the so-called experts give their reasons for the causes and effects that brought us to this point, what really matters is what we believe and what we do with it.

Many individuals take what someone else says as an absolute road map to exactly the same results. At the core of Brutally Honest is the belief that we cannot simply follow exactly what others do and expect the same results unless every factor is identical. I'm not saying experts or authors are lying or misrepresenting matters; I'm saying that what works for Olympic athletes to get them gold medals does not necessarily work for a divorced parent with no job but with children to raise.

So what do we do when confronted with such a situation or any other scenario? The answer lies in the process of ongoing positive absorption (OPA), which states that we should continually concentrate on absorbing information from as many positive sources as we can.

This system is different from saturation, which is what Olympic athletes engage in when they fully engage in training. No one can replicate another individual no matter how hard he or she tries. Many people wrote books about their experiences flipping properties and making a lot of money. Others bought their books and tried to follow their examples. Some succeeded, but others didn't. Exercise and diet books are other examples of this; some achieve the results these books promise while others don't. Those who have unlimited time to exercise have a chance of success greater than do those with time constraints—working two jobs to support five children and living in Iceland. That said, if the person in Iceland has access to a gym between his or her jobs and the other has physical disabilities, does that not change the odds?

As opposed to having only one be-all-do-all method in which we saturate ourselves, I recommend we seek information from as many credible sources as possible to match up with our unique circumstances, skills, opportunities, availability, and other factors. That allows for a more well-rounded perspective. That's OPA. This process allows us to always keep an open mind for additional perspectives, ideas, and options. By its nature, the process will keep us growing as we accumulate more information, and not just any information but positive information.

What I offer to you, my clients, family, and friends in this book is advice I believe can assist in many areas. As mentioned above, however, though I feel strongly about it and have used most of it successfully in my own, my family's, and my clients' lives, it too is but one source of information for you to consider when assessing your life.

When clients come to see me, we talk about what brought them to me. We consider the past, assess the present, and develop their goals. We start to develop a road map to help them get from where they are to where they want to be. Often in the beginning stages of our meeting, they are riddled with fear, doubt, low self-esteem, and many other limiting beliefs. They cannot see past the present painful circumstances. As we develop the path forward, I help them overcome their limiting beliefs and begin to paint a picture for them of what a compelling future could look like. I tell them that while I know they have difficulty thinking about anything but their current, painful circumstances, they should at least leave open the possibility that a brighter future exists; that hope is necessary for their moving forward and making change. Change does not happen overnight, but it starts with that first positive belief and step in the right direction.

To contribute to your OPA, I respectfully offer you things that have contributed to my and my family's, my clients', and my friends' OPA. I encourage you to utilize some or all the ideas and match them up to what you can do and like to do. I'll give you an assortment of things to think of that have provided much-needed value throughout my life. Keep in mind that you should use these as a resource and consideration only. While you may find that you agree with many of them, you may disagree with others. That's okay. The core of Brutally Honest is considering many sources. After doing so, you match things that resonate with you and your capabilities, interests, personality, and the like. I hope these will inspire and help you so you can pay forward what you learned while adding positive, unique things to the world that help others.

The following are but a few suggestions to supercharge your efforts to sur-thrive in Generation Now. Any one of the following snippets could be and in most cases are the subject of complete books, but I offer them as snapshots. If you enjoy what you read, I encourage you to delve further into the topics in books, seminars, podcasts, and so on.

Likewise, some of the following may not be possible based on your unique circumstances. You might not have a wife or a husband or children, but you might have a significant other and family members or friends. Just be creative, have fun, and change your life and those of the people closest to you. To add to your enjoyment and success, share this information with others. Read through it together and do the exercises with family and friends. Challenge each other to make improvement while acting as each other's accountability partner.

1. Family First

My life revolves around my family, the innermost circle of my personal bull's-eye. All else spreads from there. We learn, share, grow, support, and love each other unconditionally, the purest form of love. No matter what's happening in our lives, we know we can always feel safe and secure with each other—not be judged but supported. Whether we have rough or smooth days, whether we are sick or feeling great, whether the economy is inclining or declining, whether tragedy or elation comes, we look forward to sharing with each other in an environment in which we know we can be ourselves and be accepted for who we are. We use the word *love* liberally—we tell each other every day that we love each other.

How's your family? Is it strong? Is it in turmoil? Are you connected with each other? Are there some who need forgiveness or from whom you seek forgiveness? Are there some you have been meaning to say something to? Do you freely tell your family members that you love them? What have you wanted to do for, say to, or show those who matter most to you? Why not do so today?

You may have close family members you wanted to thank, forgive, or say "I'm sorry" to for things in the past but they have passed on, and you live with regret wishing you had just one more opportunity to speak with them. That happens to us all; we shouldn't kick ourselves because it's impossible to be all things to all people. It's always easier looking back and asking all the what-ifs. It would be nice if life were that easy. We could also look back and relive example after example of wonderful things we've done for countless people; it's all about what we focus on.

I am proofreading this section well after I wrote it in the wake of my using an applicable example for the last two weeks. I have used the following example with family friends, LaMonaca Law clients, and team members. It's simple but powerful:

> If I were in a pitch-black room with five people to my right and to my left and I have a flashlight, they will see only what I shine the beam on. If that beam is focused on a negative thing, that's what they'll see. Likewise, if I

focus it on a positive item, they too will see only that. I could also change the beam from tight to wide to allow them to see many items all at once.

—Gregory LaMonaca

The above example is powerful in that it describes how we perceive life. We focus on where the light is aimed. That is how the news media, businesses, and everyone attempt to influence us. Realize that we control our flashlights and can choose where to shine them. As you direct your light, you'll influence what others see. That is powerful. Use it wisely!

Not everyone has a loving, caring, and supportive family; people may be going through some rough times where they disconnect with one or more. Many of my clients at LaMonaca Law come to us with these situations. Those going through divorce clearly experience this loss as the one most trusted and closest to them is now at the other extreme. Custody is one of the most significant issues troubled parents face. Most parents would fight harder for their children than for anything else. At these moments, I encourage them to find other family members on whom they can lean for support.

You can shine your flashlight at all the things you could have or should have done, but don't kick yourself for missed opportunities. Instead, focus the beam on what's in front of you. Do something today that you can control. Whom can you call today in your family to in fact make a difference, mend old wounds, or take your relationship with to the next level? What family members are literally under your roof whom you can make new, extraordinary moments with? There's time right now for you to create lifelong memories. What *will* you do today to make a difference?

2. Make Your Spouse or Significant Other Your Partner

My wife is my best friend, my most trusted confidant, and an unconditional partner. My world starts with her and my children and expands from there to other family and friends. There are not hers and mine; there are only ours. We share almost everything. We plan together, consult with each other, make decisions together, have joint bank accounts, own property together, and share all other areas of our lives.

Of course, this does not mean we don't enjoy separate hobbies and friends, have disagreements, and many other things that make up our unique identities, but we are a team, best friends. Some say married couples should cohabitate but separate many things—their lives, bank accounts, goals, and such. I'm sure many successful relationships work that way, but as a family law attorney, I note one issue that shows up consistently in divorce cases—separate goals, values, and lives. A marriage is a unity that's not consistent with living separate lives.

Marriage is a team, not a place for two coexisting units. No winning team is based on two dynamic individuals doing their own things independently of each other. How many professional football or basketball teams have had superstars who individually led in many categories of stats but that ended up in last place? Successful marriages or partnerships do not last where there is one MVP and one benchwarmer.

I'm a devoted Philadelphia sports team fanatic, and I think Terrell Owens, TO, was one of the most talented wide receivers ever. From the first play of the season featuring Donavan McNabb throwing a length-of-field touchdown pass, Eagles fans were in heaven. Through superhuman efforts and the use of a hyperbaric chamber, an athlete whose injury would have sidelined any other for a season got better for the Super Bowl. Fast-forward to where TO let his ego get the best of him, rebelled against his coach and team, and was ultimately traded. What a waste. Many years later, he looks back on this time and regrets doing it. He acknowledged his faults but too late. In life, we don't get a chance to rewind and get another chance. But we can at any time reevaluate our choices and correct our courses.

Allen Iverson, one of the greatest Philadelphia 76er of all time and one of the greatest to play the game, landed in the Hall of Fame. Despite his size, he could do things on a court perhaps rivaled only by Michael Jordan's moves. Unbelievable talent. But like TO, he let his ego get to him and believed that he was better than the team and that he didn't need to practice, and he fought Coach Larry Brown and the organization. He got in criminal trouble, family problems, and the like. Today, he's broke. He admits all his faults, speaks of Larry Brown as a father figure, and regrets his actions. His speech as he was inducted into the Hall of Fame is legendary. I recommend you watch it online.

In any relationship, there needs to be separate identities, goals, aspirations, and things that make each individual feel unique that they contribute to the relationship. Combined, the whole is worth more than the sum of its parts. Any successful relationship takes effort, planning, work, evaluation, reevaluation, and nurturing. It is a continual learning experience that when cultivated, appreciated, and respected is perhaps one of the greatest things in life.

Contrarily, one of the big factors that contributes to most of the divorce cases I handle is when one spouse exercises power or control over the other and eventually takes away that spouse's uniqueness and changes the partnership into a dictatorship. While dictatorships may work in the short term, most if not all will lead to destruction.

It may be too late for some of you to go back and undo something that may have led to the breakup of a relationship or a marriage. In these cases, is it appropriate to perhaps tell that individual you are sorry for your part in that breakup? If so, and if it can be done in a positive manner, doing that may go a long way to breaking down some chains that have been holding you back. Perhaps you're thinking about a current relationship and what you have inappropriately done. Would apologizing for that help get things back on track? When was the last time you really asked your partner, "How was your day?" and meant it? Do you express love in a way your partner wants or in a way you want? Is your relationship purely physical, or is there a component of compassion, empathy, care, and other forms of unconditional love?

When was the last time you told your partner, "I love you"? When was the last time you showed love in a form that was not robotic, predictable, or expected? When was the last time you surprised him or her with something over the top or unexpected? When was the last time you were present in the moment and enjoying everything you have in your relationship as opposed to wishing what you could have had or taking your spouse for granted?

We can all improve our physical, emotional, and spiritual selves, and our partners can too, but instead of wishing or hoping that our partners improve in this or that area, we should revel in their unique attributes. The media bombard us with suggestions as to how we should look, act, be, and think. In my flashlight example earlier, I described the media shining their lights on what they want us to see, but that's not reality. Regardless of whether you agree with what they are showing you, they are systematically embedding in you what they want you to see. If you take a moment to evaluate what's right in front of you, you might find that you already have the greatest partner.

I idolize Monica. We met at age fourteen in freshman year of high school, and then it was freshman dance, soph hop, junior and senior proms, four years driving to and from West Chester University, and thirty-seven years together. She's the center of my universe. It seems that unconditional love is the highest form of love, but she eclipses that many times over. It is not me and she but we. We have been with each other through some of life's greatest pleasures and serious and challenging times.

Like other couples, we argue, say things out of anger, upset each other, make mistakes, and disagree, but we always have respect for each other and certainty that through it all is unconditional love and the knowledge that whatever we face together will indeed pass. We apologize, talk through it, learn from it, and move on. Healthy marriages and relationships experience these types of events. What thriving relationships have that fleeting ones do not are mechanisms in place to ensure that not if but when bad times occur, there are ways to bring things back to a healthy state.

In my law practice, I see far too many couples who do not have such mechanisms to keep their marriages on course, so they go nuclear and threaten divorce constantly, go over the top to insult or demean their partners, take to drugs or alcohol, have affairs, or do any number of harmful things to destroy their partners. And their children suffer the fallout from their relationship's destruction consciously or unconsciously.

Successful relationships are partnerships. What can you do today to improve your relationship with your spouse or significant other? If you are not in a relationship, what would you need to do to create a loving, lasting relationship?

3. Seek Mentors

Despite your level of knowledge and education, you can always benefit from developing one or more mentors, those you can call or meet with to ask questions about work, school, life, finances, or any other subject in which their expertise exceeds yours. The concept of modeling embodies this type of plan. You can spend hours, days, and weeks reading, researching, and fumbling through countless items seeking an answer to something, or you can find others who have already done what you want to do and simply ask them to help you find the answer.

Long-term relationships can develop out of trust and respect between mentors and mentees, and each can learn from the other. Be sure to always attempt to add value to your mentors and never take advantage of the relationship or their time. Most people whom you ask for assistance will be flattered by the asking and will genuinely want to assist you.

This one fact can make a radical difference in your life—somewhere, there is one, two, or perhaps thousands or even millions of people who have achieved what you want to achieve. You can't contact all of them, and not all you contact will be willing to help you, but that still leaves you with a large list of people among whom you'll certainly find some who will assist you and feel personally fulfilled by doing so. Grasp the importance of this paragraph and you'll eliminate a major obstacle to reaching your goals.

This self-imposed obstacle individuals create becomes no longer an obstacle. When you add the endless reach of the internet, your potential to find a mentor is now worldwide and within a few clicks. A simple Google search will open you up to infinite data about whatever issue you may have—websites, articles, podcasts, videos on YouTube, and many other sources—and the names of those behind the data. How tough would it be to send an email to someone requesting advice? Yes, I know some won't respond, but others will; 97 percent of individuals won't send out that initial email, but 3 percent will look past their self-imposed barriers and do something about it. Where do you fall?

In addition to individuals are countless professionals whose businesses can give you help in many areas, and you'll get what you pay for. There are many free-resource sites as well as people who will give you certain degrees of advice, but even in a mentoring situation, there will be a limit as to what any one person can do. LaMonaca Law represents individuals who have sought us out for advice and representation in divorce, custody, child abduction, and abuse cases among many others. We work with everyone to craft a custom-tailored plan and team to match his or her needs, goals, and budgets.

In addition to live mentors, consider all those you can meet through their books, audios, videos, podcasts, TV, and the internet. You can obtain information on just about anything almost instantly. If there's something you're looking to do, you'll find many such resources that deal with it. Every day, I read educational books, listen to motivational audios in the car, watch educational programs on TV, and listen to free podcasts.

Technology is evolving exponentially and at warp speed. Things that took decades to happen now happen in weeks. For example, as I was proofreading this section well after I first wrote it, my list of items above had expanded to include watching live videos on Facebook and Periscope. Both services now allow you to view live individuals and interact with them. Unlike YouTube, on which can watch countless and useful videos, you now can watch those you follow streaming live video and ask them questions in real time. How cool is that? I can only dream about where technology is heading.

Beyond this there are also many old-school, tried-and-true groups you can join, including Rotary, Toastmasters, and chambers of commerce that are filled with people seeking and willing to give guidance. For over seventeen years, I belonged to a group called BNI (Business Networking International), the world's largest referral network. We met once a week to interact with, learn from, and grow with each other. Four of our LaMonaca Law team members are currently active members in four chapters.

If there is not a group that fits your needs, think about creating one. Years back, I created a group entitled DVEF, the Delaware Valley Entrepreneurial Forum, and chose nine others to join. We met once a month in an educational forum to help each other. All of us were business owners and sizeable investors in stocks, real estate, or the like and had a certain minimum net worth; these were successful people, and each focused on assisting the others. We weren't there to drum up business from each other but to help each other and support everyone. So many extra ears, eyes, and mouths helped us all stay on track.

Creating the group cost me nothing more than time in preparing introductory materials and time to meet. Not a bad return on my investment to get the assistance of nine diverse, passionate, successful professionals who all wanted to learn, grow, and help the others. Whom can you call right now and form a similar group with? You'd be surprised at how a group of the right people can help you overcome obstacles and guide you along your path.

The ideas above create almost instant advice and help in the areas where you need assistance removing a self-imposed barrier. There exist at any given time countless mentors real or virtual who can help you as you navigate the path.

Do you believe you have all the answers? How many people have you tried to genuinely help who refused to listen and didn't even give you a chance to assist them? Many of us go through life fearing that accepting help from others means we are weak and will be perceived as not knowing what we're doing. On the contrary, smart people rely on the right people to help them succeed. Those who seek out mentors tend to be more successful, save a lot of time, and are more fulfilled than those who rely only on themselves. Napoleon Hill touted the benefit of mastermind groups many years ago—the whole is more than the sum of its parts.

Whom can you contact today to ask to mentor you in a specific area or concern? What books, audios, podcasts, videos, and online interactive services can you obtain to help and guide you? What other free resources exist right now that you can study and learn from? Stop here—literally—go on the internet, and spend an hour discovering what free items are right in front of you that can help you in areas in which you want assistance. Commit and allocate time each day to do these things and you will find yourself empowered and fulfilled.

4. Be a Mentor

In life, you can't always take; you must give back to be complete. That is one of my main objectives in writing and publishing this book. In this regard, just as you should seek out mentors to help you get where you want to be, so too should you always attempt to help others get to where they want to be. It doesn't matter how far you went in school or whether you possess advanced degrees. We all have unique characteristics and talents that make us who we are and that could give others an advantage they don't possess. By taking a few or more people under your wings, you can positively affect their lives and the world.

I have assisted and am assisting many people—students, colleagues, friends, family, clients, team members, and others. Help others, and you will also help yourself learn, grow, and do your part to make the world better. We all face obstacles in our lives. I bet you look on the hurdles you've cleared as lessons learned even if some were unintentional while others were planned and sought out.

We learn in various ways. One is through researching a topic and applying what we learn. This gives us one level of knowledge. If you add photos and videos to the lesson, it increases your chance of retrieval and benefitting from them. If you attend a live seminar where you are present while someone is speaking, you add more. At the pinnacle, however, is the concept of experiential learning; this is where you interact with others and fully participate in the learning activity together.

Your goal as a mentor is to impart useful knowledge to someone you are mentoring. Using the various techniques above, you will find that each has its place. At LaMonaca Law, one of my primary functions is to teach, guide, and lead some of the brightest individuals who make up our team at the firm. I teach the same way I learn. I incorporate what I learn from books, podcasts, CDs, and other vehicles any one day into my vocabulary that I then use with everyone I meet that day. In addition to simply relaying words, I use stories to convey the messages. Through these stories, I get animated, use tone, inflection, passion, and gestures to help others visualize what I'm trying to convey. And then I'll have other team members sit in meetings I have with other team members and clients to allow them to observe live and in person the various methods I use and their results. This is also used in a courtroom where through our team approach, I will often have one or more other team members there with me. This is by far the best form of full-out experiential learning. I learn from them as much as they learn from me.

In December 2017, I met with each team member at my firm for several hours. We discussed how I could best assist them, what their personal goals were for 2018, and how they were evolving. I shared with them cutting-edge ideas to help them succeed not just at the law firm but also in life. After completing these one-on-one meetings, I met again with each member of our firm leadership team. We discussed focused examples of how they—we—could improve as leaders with our families, clients, and each other. I spent over sixty hours mentoring our team members at LaMonaca Law, my second family.

As a mentor, you have the privilege of sharing your knowledge with others. You also will save your mentees thousands of hours of trial and error by giving them shortcuts to success. By giving them visuals by way of real-life stories, you will be solidifying in them information they can use immediately.

I'm a big proponent of a strong work ethic, learning by doing, and making mistakes. By doing things, failing, and learning from that, we improve. In an ideal world, mentors would give their mentees useful information so that they wouldn't make catastrophic mistakes but allow them to find their own ways.

The mentors' role is to periodically check in with their mentees to see how they are progressing, check their progress, answer questions, and continue to guide them down their paths. Note that guiding them is different from doing their work for them. Too many young people expect things to be handed to them without their having earned them. Many parents make the mistake of doing everything for their children and spoil them in the process. Parents should love their children unconditionally, but that doesn't mean doing everything for them.

Among the greatest things we can give our children are a strong work ethic and useable skills both physical and mental. If we are successful in this most important role, we will increase the chances that when they find themselves in situations where they will need to make decisions, they will be the right decisions.

I tell my clients who are living together during difficult times that their children are sponges; they soak up everything they see and hear and are developing their blueprints for life. When they witness fighting, arguments, demeaning talk, violence, alcohol, drugs, or any other of the countless issues that come up in troubled marriages, they consciously and unconsciously learn what it's like to be a man or a woman and how to act in various situations. Often, children of divorce take on many of these same traits in their relationships, but children raised in loving, caring, respectful environments pick up those traits.

I have mentored and advised thousands of clients, family members, and friends. I believe it is my obligation to give back and help others get to their next levels in life. I am extremely passionate about my role and obligations as a mentor. Nothing gives me greater pleasure than helping others navigate this wonderful ride called life. When I do, I am in my element. When you have learned tasks and have been blessed with skill sets, I believe you should give these gifts to others much the same way they were given to you.

Recently, I met with a family member who had just graduated college and was looking for guidance and advice. I gladly carved out some time in the middle of an otherwise hectic day that begun at about four in the morning. I got to work at five, planned for the many tasks I had to handle, answered countless emails, returned calls from troubled clients who needed guidance, and met with two new clients. He and I met at noon, and I listened to his situation, aspirations, and goals and his plans to achieve them. I suggested many things that he could do to supercharge his journey, including several books I felt would best relate to his current situation and get him thinking more long term. He took detailed notes and asked great questions. Given that my clients pay me hundreds of dollars an hour, I compare my time with those I mentor to the time I could have spent with clients, but I never begrudge the time if I believe my mentees genuinely want the information I offer and will do the hard work necessary to put that information to work for themselves. With that criterion, I gladly stick by them and do anything I can for them.

Many people have sought me out after reading one of my books or pulled me aside after seeing me in court and asked for my advice. In this economy, requests for my assistance and guidance have been insanely high. What I find is that 97 percent of those who come to me in panicked states—nervous, out of options, fearful, or about to lose their families, businesses, and so on—listen intently to my advice, but only a few follow through with it. Most people want quick fixes for their problems, but life doesn't work that way.

You have to work hard and be diligent, focused, and intent on raising your standards so you can overcome obstacles, get leverage and momentum, and begin to get to your next level. More important, you need to be willing to do whatever is necessary to achieve the results you want and take one step at a time down the long and rocky road called life.

Your time is precious and finite, so you must focus your efforts and be willing to help others overcome their limitations and obstacles and do whatever is necessary to get through the barriers that stand in their way to your compelling future.

Whom can you help today with your unique talents and gifts?

5. Reduce Your Debt

Many of the problems that gave rise to the recent economic crisis had to do with our having too much debt or taking unnecessary risks (mortgages, HELOs, etc.). Most Americans have far too much credit card debt and other ways they risk their futures for instant gratification today. Record bankruptcies, foreclosures, and credit lines frozen or revoked underscore this epidemic. By paying with cash, living within our means, avoiding overextending ourselves, and paying down our debts one item at a time, we will be in a much better place. By doing this, yes, we will be different. We will be in the minority.

Take for example paying off your mortgage. Many pundits preach that mortgage debt is good as we get tax benefits. Think of the logic, however. Why would I want to spend a dollar to save twenty-eight cents, give or take in taxes? How great would it be if we had no debt? I realize that for many, that's a pipe dream, but it's possible with planning, a change in lifestyle, attacking debt, time, monitoring, and commitment. Some things are beyond our control (health, losing a job because of downsizing, etc.), but we can focus on what we can control.

I debate this point often with individuals who seem to be over their heads in student loans, mortgages, credit card, and other form of debt. I recognize this feeling of being overwhelmed. I worked full time through college and law school, but I too had a large student loan debt. Fast-forward to today—I no longer have this debt. From the beginning, Monica and I developed a joint plan to attack that debt, and most important, we worked that plan one day at a time, one payment at a time while sacrificing many things we wanted to do or buy to work toward our future. I counsel individuals faced with overwhelming debt to do the same—systematically chop away at debt.

I have learned that financial problems cause many divorces because of spouses simply not being on the same page, not communicating with each other, and having separate goals, ideals, and views on spending and saving. The perfect storm happens when both parties agree to spend, spend, and spend. Clients look at me as if I have two heads when this issue comes up and I candidly tell them to stop spending. Life changes and quickly. If times are good, if the economy is booming (as it is now in January 2018), if jobs are secure, both spouses are working, and so on, their ability and willingness to spend on nonessentials is greater. But when the economy inevitably cycles down and life throws a curve in terms of health or employment, there needs to also be a mind shift and a new perspective. I heard a stat this morning that most Americans have only $1,000 saved; they're only one tragic life event away from becoming destitute.

We need to have a backup plan in place that can instantly spring into effect when life challenges us so we can patch the leak in the ship to keep it afloat. Debt reduction is immediate and certain. It's that simple—stop spending on all but the essentials—food, shelter, and clothing. If you went out to lunch, stop! Dinners out, stop! Paid trips, stop! Movies and concerts, stop! Massages and spa trips, stop! Trips, stop! I can't believe how many people come to me for advice and tell me just how bad things are, how much debt they have, how bad life is for them, and in the same sentence say how they just bought this, went out to dinner, took trips, and the like. They defend themselves to the end saying, "But my case is different." They say that there is no way they can change, as there is nothing to change. However, a quick analysis of their day may show that they get up each day, drive to Starbucks and spend three to eight dollars on a coffee mocha guava latte or whatever the drink of the day is, and later, they spend another five to twenty dollars on lunch. I give this one example of what I can typically do in a few questions to open their eyes to what they are spending. I suggest they bring coffee from home along with a brown-bag lunch. I tell them to add to their savings by shopping for clothes less frequently. In almost every case, there are ways to save additional sums of money if people simply looked for them and willingly sacrificed for their and their families' futures.

Financial crises will hit again, and life will continue to throw curveballs, so don't think otherwise. You should and must plan now. Over the years, our family has picked classic books to read together. I'd get four copies so we could all read and discuss it. One such book was Napoleon Hill's *Think and Grow Rich*, a phenomenal book written in the 1930s. I have read it at least a dozen times, and it grounds me each time I do. The interesting thing is that though he wrote it after the 1929 stock market crash, it applies to the rough economic times Americans went through in recent years before the current boom.

There will be another crash—it's not an if, but a when. If you bury your head in the sand and pretend it won't happen, you're doing a severe disservice to yourself and your family. You are blessed to have the past as a guide. More important, educate your children from the time they can start processing information on financial literacy.

I recommend having at least six if not nine months or a year of a safety and security fund in a liquid account. This fund is not to be used for trips, dinners, shoes, or new golf clubs; it is to be tapped only when emergencies or crises occur. Knowing you have assets ready to assist your family should an emergency arise will give you peace of mind and allow you to live comfortably for the period you have set aside money for.

If you think you can't do that, look inside yourself and determine what's more important—going out to a restaurant or securing the financial safety of your family? That sounds harsh, but such reflection is part of the Brutally Honest system. Stop making excuses and take action. I guarantee that if you make an honest assessment of each purchase you made just last week, you'll find you've wasted countless dollars that could have been used for your emergency fund, to pay down debt, and save for your future.

You may have heard the phrase "Work hard and play hard." That's correct. There's nothing wrong with playing hard, having fun, and spending money on relaxing, fun activities. The point is that you must first work hard to earn the right to play hard. Some of those reading this book are financially secure while others may be in dire straits. Some may be in their golden years while others are in their teens. Clearly, the earlier you start saving, the better, and it's never too late to start saving and training your children to do so too.

In addition to the safety and security fund are a few things that will give you greater comfort when crises come than to be debt free. Think about it—if you lose your job, a health crisis hits, or you face another one of life's surprise calamities, how good will you feel knowing that other than your basic needs such as food, electric, taxes, and so forth, you don't have any other payments?

Again, many readers will say that's great for others but not for them because they consider that impossible. I tell them that if they keep that attitude, they'll be correct. If they spent even half as much time focusing on the solution as they do on making excuses, they could get on the right path. I ask them what steps they have taken to move forward and watch as they stare downward without anything to say.

Step one is to put together a budget of what it will take to provide the basics for your family. Keep written track of everything you and your spouse spend for an entire week and review it together. Make it a fun family project. Besides the Starbucks and the going out to lunch I mentioned above, do you go to the movies instead of playing board games or going to parks? Have you ever spent a weekend at home pretending to be on vacation?

Your plan to reduce debt must be a family plan. It does little good when one member is onboard and the others do not care. This single issue has contributed immensely to many of the divorces I see. One spouse focuses on debt reduction while the other speaks a good game but doesn't contribute to the income or continues to buy, buy, buy.

Inventory your household possessions and determine which could be sold in a garage sale or on eBay. If your whole family does this, you'll find countless ways to save and have fun in the process. What better way to teach your children the values of saving by converting items that were accumulating dust into money that can pay down debt?

Okay, you've done all the above, saved a lot of money, and raised money from other jobs, sales, and the like. You created your six- to nine-month safety and security fund, so now what? It's time focus relentlessly on paying down your debt. Begin with paying down the credit card debt that charges the highest interest rate. One card at a time, pay down the balance with the extra savings you've found. Once that card is paid off, take those extra savings and pay the next one—and so on. And I recommend then getting rid of your credit cards because they're poison. Did you ever hear of cash? You know, that green-and-white paper you can use to buy things? What a concept—buying things only when you have the money to pay for them. I'm being facetious but factual. The attitude today is that you don't need cash to buy anything; you charge it, go into debt, and become instantly gratified.

The hot topics as I write this in 2018 are bitcoin and other cryptocurrencies. This attitude is injected into our society by advertising of all sorts, and it targets our kids as well. Credit card companies camp out at college campuses like sharks looking for prey. Student after student takes the bait and signs up for the cards to get instant prizes for doing so. What they end up with, however, is a lifelong addiction to debt. Don't let your kids fall prey to that. Teach them by example that the way to get something they want is to save and sacrifice until they have the money to buy it. If they need a card, make sure it's a debit card with limits. The concept of delayed gratification has been lost. The internet has fueled the need for instant gratification. You cannot fall prey to this. Real simple— use cash. If you don't have it, don't buy it. Novel, huh?

After you pay off your credit card debt, attack all other sources of debt, including car loans, student loans, other creditors, and eventually your mortgage. What may seem impossible to you right now starts with a willingness to change that translates into a conviction, a written plan, and that first crucial step toward change.

People tell Monica and me, "You don't understand. You don't have the same situation as I do with massive student loans and debt." I have used or done almost everything in this book successfully —it's not just theory. Where Monica and I are today is the sum of many years of working hard to develop and follow a plan, save, save more, and sacrifice pleasures every step of the way to solidifying our futures. We have no concept what it was like to party at college; we worked full time in college and law school as I mentioned. We drove to school and then to work; we then drove home to study half the night.

We were recently driving by a Wawa near West Chester University with Alyssa and Gregory. We laughed and joked about how Monica and I would stop at that Wawa as we left school on our way to work to buy what we called weenies and cheeps—our lunch. It was a ninety-nine-cent special consisting of two hot dogs and a bag of potato chips. That and water in thermoses were the makings of an awesome date as we devoured them on the way to work.

We worked for minimum wage, confronted medical issues and deaths in our families, and faced student loans, world problems, and the like as a team. After law school, we got married and worked together to pay down debt. We started a family, and we committed to working, speaking, planning, learning, and growing together.

I fondly and vividly remember in the early years of our marriage Monica and I lying in bed eating cheese and crackers (otherwise called dinner) while reading aloud together Suze Orman's *The Nine Steps to Financial Freedom* (1997). We had fun doing each lesson. One was saving all our extra change every day, and we saved hundreds of dollars that way. Since then, Monica and I and later Alyssa and Gregory have read hundreds of books together. As we did, we learned, evolved, put into practice the lessons we learned, and strengthened our family bond while instilling lifelong values and fundamental principles that assisted our entire family and generations to come.

No one just arrives; anything of significance takes planning, sacrifice, and work, more work, and yet more work. While it would be nice to have things handed to us without having to do anything, there is price to pay for everything. Likewise, working together with Monica and later Alyssa and Gregory has provided us some of the greatest times in life I wouldn't trade for anything!

How can you change your lifestyle today to start down the path of living without debt so your future will be secure?

6. Never Stop Growing

When you stop growing, you die. School is just one form of education; my life is filled with multiple sources of enrichment. I read voraciously about many subjects filled with self-improvement. I listen to self-help audios on my iPhone and iPad in my car and in bed—I take every opportunity I can to learn. I read magazines on many topics as well as newspapers, I attend seminars, write (as I am doing here), and engage in an assortment of learning opportunities. I meet with my mentors and mentor others. I watch DVDs, review You Tube videos on subjects of interest, and listen to a multitude of podcasts. Much of the TV we watch focuses on business, entrepreneurship, and other ways to grow. Learning does not stop after formal education and certainly is not the only way we grow. By reading this, you're taking a step in the right direction. Ensure that you take steps each day to continue your education.

Many years ago, I stumbled upon a book on personal development entitled *Unlimited Power* by Anthony Robbins. In life, things tend to happen to us with no rhyme or reason. I can't remember how I came upon this book, but I did when I was an impressionable young individual starting out into the wild, confusing, and rapidly changing world, so the book came at a good time. Tony was the king of the infomercial; he commanded late-night TV with his promotion of his audio program (some of you may remember cassettes ... and there are those who will recall eight tracks and records) entitled "Personal Power." I read his book cover to cover and was captivated. I purchased his thirty-day cassette program on Personal Power, which at the time, was a sizeable investment for a student earning minimum wage. As he said, it became a must as opposed to a should; it wasn't a matter of if I purchased it but of how and when I could. Like a kid waiting to open his first present on Christmas, I anxiously awaited the box to arrive. When it did, I immediately jumped into the first tape. It was as if I were conversing with a good friend. I listened to all the cassettes and completed all the activities. Since that time, I did that exact seminar many times. It is very satisfying to review the workbooks from each of these times to show the progress I made in between each. That began my lifelong passion for reading, listening to, viewing, and attending personal-development seminars.

I've since read, listened to, and viewed everything Tony has put out. Monica and I attended his "Unleash the Power Within" seminar and walked on burning coals as one of countless life-changing events during the four-day seminar. The result was that Tony became my first mentor in the field of personal development. The pinnacle of this relationship was in October 2012 when my wife and I were invited to attend a rare appearance to be one of the featured guests to interact with Tony and share my story on QVC, the nation's largest seller of on-air products. What an opportunity! I was thrilled and nervous. Not much gets me nervous as I regularly appear before judges in high-pressure cases. There, however, I was getting the opportunity to meet and even interact with my mentor. It was exciting and humbling.

I was invited by one of QVC's top on-air hosts. Years back, I had represented her spouse in a contentious custody matter, and I spoke with her at length during the many court recesses. She shared with me many obstacles she had faced growing up that had affected her at times. I gave her advice to use in moving forward to confront the obstacles that were holding her back. We spoke at length by phone after that as she evolved through this to continue to be an amazing, accomplished individual.

Over the years, we stayed in touch. They say no good deed goes unpunished. As it turned out, she was the on-air host many times with Tony as he came to promote his various products. During one such time, she shared with him my personal story of overcoming obstacles, Brutally Honest, and how I assisted her using these principles. She shared my use of his products over the years and my giving credit to him for getting me started and through many personal challenges I'd had. She emailed me and said she had something exciting to tell me. I was shocked when she relayed that to me. There would be a first-time studio audience at an upcoming Tony Appearance at QVC. The audience was to comprise a select few personal guests who had testimonials, with Monica and I being two of them.

As time grew closer to the appearance, I imagined I'd receive specific instructions, but that didn't occur. I reached out to my contact and determined she was on vacation, but she said she would put me in touch with the person who would make it happen. Three weeks away, two weeks, one week—no contact. I didn't want to push the issue, but I did send another email and learned Monica and I would get tickets for a specific date and time.

We headed to the studio without knowing whether I would speak or simply be a guest. I rehearsed countless options of what I could say if asked to speak. Thankfully, as an attorney, I was well practiced in such activities. When appearing on behalf of a client, I always have plans A, B, and C as I never knew exactly how a judge will rule or react. I had to be able to change directions and still be compelling.

We anxiously drove to the studio as these possibilities shuffled through my head. We got our tickets, went through security, and waited in line with about thirty people. I still wondered what to expect. Someone ahead of me asked, "Are you Greg LaMonaca?" I couldn't see who had asked that. We were escorted to our seats with no further information. We sat in their amphitheater with about fifty people. I had two thoughts going through my head. One was that I hoped I wouldn't be asked to speak. I had researched the QVC site and learned it typically had seventy million viewers. My other thought, however, was that if I were asked to speak, I'd have the opportunity of a lifetime to publicly thank my mentor.

I saw a producer with a clipboard giving some people instructions on when they would be speaking. I saw her list at one point; my name was not on it. The show began as Tony ran from behind us down the aisle and high-fiving me as I was on the end. It was amazing watching Tony genuinely interacting with the host, the on-air audience, and taking questions from viewers and the audience members the producer had spoken to. After forty minutes of the one-hour show, I was convinced I wouldn't be asked to speak. Monica and I enjoyed the show, and my heart rate went back to normal.

Then it happened. With ten minutes left, a different producer came over and told me that they had saved me for last and that I would be speaking in about a minute. She asked me to stand at a certain spot for my chance to speak with my mentor. What a moment!

As I stood on the spot with seconds to go before speaking in front of what turned out to be one hundred million viewers, I experienced an unusual peacefulness and calm. Instead of this overwhelming, anxious experience, it was as if I were about to have a conversation with one of my closest friends. The host said she was going to the audience. The interviewer said to me, "Tell me a little about your life and how Tony has changed it."

For the next several minutes, I talked about my life's journey and how I had first read Tony's *Unlimited Power* book. How I had listened to all his products, attended his seminars with my "beautiful wife Monica," whom I introduced and pointed out (To this day, we all get a kick out of watching the close-up of Monica as she gave a perfect princess wave with her beautiful smile.) I told him how we had a picture of our daughter in her crib with one of Tony's books and how I had listened to his tapes as I fought to recover from paralysis and the many surgeries that followed. How I had used his principles to develop along with a friend the Brutally Honest system, the book that followed—*The Brutally Honest Life Management Journal*—and how I used those principles to help all our divorce and custody clients. How he was a mentor to me much as his mentor, Jim Rohn, had been to him. I expressed my condolences to Tony for the loss of Jim, who had passed away the year before. Tears came to his eyes, and he asked if he could give me a hug. I walked to meet him, and in front of a million viewers, he gave me a kiss and a hug and told me I was amazing. Words cannot express the joy I felt.

Tony went back to the stage as I took my seat and said, "You're why I do all this crazy stuff. I'm grateful for you sharing that, to know that all those people told you what you couldn't do, and to go through all of that physical challenge, and to see you today contributing to other people, not just taking care of yourself. I mean, that's what life's about. In the end, what you get won't make you happy, but who you become and what you give will make you very happy. Congratulations." As he said that, he wiped a tear from his eye.

That experience was one of the most amazing experiences of my life. After the show, his personal assistant came out and said Tony wanted to meet us. My wife and I were escorted into the hallway, where we met

Tony. He was larger than life; he towered over us. He embraced Monica and me, and we talked as if we were close friends. He is beyond genuine.

A funny moment happened when Monica showed him the photo of our daughter in the crib with his book. He laughed and asked if he could keep it. At that point, Monica's Momma Bear came out; she asked Tony if we could send him a copy as that was our only copy. He laughed and graciously agreed. He asked us about what seminar we were at, and we told him it was his "Unleash the Power Within." He said that we had to be his personal guests at the upcoming, weeklong, "Date with Destiny Seminar" in Palm Springs, California, in December. We were very grateful, and we thanked him for that great gift. I gave him a copy of my book wherein I wrote, "To Tony ... Thank you for being an inspiration and mentor to me throughout my life ... God Bless ... 9/16/12."

Monica and I left on cloud nine. It was one of those indelible experiences that seemed surreal. Some audience members told us how inspirational my words had been. My cell phone rang nonstop; many friends and family had seen the show. At the time of this writing, you can view the entire video of the appearance on the law firm's YouTube page or on the law firm's website, www.lamonacalaw.com.

That following December, Monica and I flew to Palm Springs and were Tony's guests at his pinnacle seminar "Date with Destiny." We spent six days along with people from seventy other countries and radically transformed our lives. Monica and I shared our magical, thirty-year journey, which we continuously share with our children as we learn and grow as a family.

Between the time I read Tony's first book many years ago through the time I met him, I have consumed thousands of books. Books are food for me; they nourish my mind and enrich my soul. They allow me to focus and constantly learn new, different, and game-changing information I use to improve my life and those of my family, friends, and clients. Tony refers to this as CANI,—Constant and Never-Ending Improvement. It sounds as if I'm a radical devotee of Tony, but it started when I stumbled upon his book many years ago. What books have you read or could read that could transform your life? I hope this book will be the one that starts you on your course toward an abundant future.

As I mentioned, in addition to books, there are audio programs on every topic imaginable. You can order them or download them and listen to them whenever you want. YouTube and podcasts offer everything you could want for free. You can buy whatever those who appeal to you are offering and even see them live at seminars. You have no excuses for not doing some of these things and thus improving your and your family's lives.

Several months after attending Tony's "Date with Destiny," Jim Grim and I attended Brendon Burchard's four-day "Experts Academy" in California. That seminar comprised people from all over the world who wanted to improve in various areas.

Your need to learn new things never stops even after your formal education does. You constantly need to improve to thrive in Generation Now. Jim Grim lived by this belief and credited the Brutally Honest system with allowing him to fight, plan, and be enlightened in life. Everyone who had the pleasure of knowing him will remember his life and legacy through the pages of this book, our first book, and the infinite pearls of wisdom, as he left so many.

Wherever the world is, strive to be several years ahead of it in your thinking and planning. You may ask, "How do I do that?" Without additional information, it may very well be impossible. If you simply float through life from one milestone to the other, you will simply be subsisting. If you're lucky, you'll get by. Chances are, however, that without preparation, you will find yourself in the company of the masses who had the rug pulled out from under them during this last economic collapse because they were not prepared and did not possess the knowledge to survive let alone thrive.

Interesting timing—as I was proofreading this book in the last week of March 2017, I remembered speaking with one of my outstanding attorneys at LaMonaca Law. She complimented me on how I had known so much about the topics we were discussing. I said to her, "I didn't just arrive. Remember when you were at my house for the 2016 LaMonaca Law fall party? Remember I showed you our new library on the lower level? I have over a thousand books there on personal development, seven hundred more upstairs in my home office, and about another five hundred elsewhere around the house. How long does it take you to read one such book?" She replied, "About a month." I said, "I can read up to three a month depending on the books. I don't just read a book. I write notes in the margin, and I have my highlighter in hand. Do the math and figure just how many years it took me to read these books. Add to that the thousands of CDs, magazines, podcasts and audiobooks I listen to in the car. I'm not lucky. I'm the sum of decades of feeding my mind with multiple sources of education."

She smiled and said, "I get it now." I hope that lesson will forever change her life. I used that example in team leadership meetings the rest of the week.

By engaging in a life that continuously feeds your mind, by reading and listening to a variety of experts in endless fields, you will find yourself prepared to get through many if not most of life's inevitable curves. Sitting back and hoping you'll be okay or believing there will never be another collapse, world crisis, illness, death in the family, or other such problems will leave you underprepared and riddled with the same anxiety that many others feel as they struggle just to subsist. They will have to rely on government handouts or assistance from others. What happens if you fail to save and invest in your future and the government runs out of money? What will you do then? The next section will help you with that.

Your reading this book tells me you are different. You are not willing to simply ride the coattails of others or sit back and hope. The simple act of reading this book and completing the exercises places you in a very small group of individuals who are exercising *Extreme Ownership* (a phenomenal book by navy SEALs Jocko Willink and Leif Babin, St. Martin's Press, 2015) of their destinies. Extreme Ownership in their words means taking 100% accountability for your actions. What can you do today to begin or continue your life's education?

7. Save and Invest

When you start writing a chapter on saving and investing, you can easily tap into some of the world's greatest thinkers, investors, financiers, and the like. There are as many different approaches as there are pundits professing to have the right approach. My thoughts in this chapter are real-life, easy to understand, and easy to follow principles that have worked. The biggest problem in investing is not what is going on in the market but instead not being in the market.

Einstein said that one of the greatest gifts we have is compound interest. Warren Buffet, one of world's best-known and wealthiest individuals, touts compound interest as one of the greatest advantages the average investor has for long-term investing. Compound interest is the process of seeing our money growing over time. While it's easy to conclude that by living through prior crashes (where our hard-earned money evaporated) that we should keep all our money in cash and in our mattresses. Conventional wisdom, however, says that over longer periods of time, having an age-appropriate, well-diversified portfolio of varying asset classes will yield positive results more often than not. I am not preaching or recommending any particular investing types. What I am suggesting is that by implementing a combination of psychology, resilience, patience, and continuous investing, your chances of financial freedom will increase exponentially. Given the meteoric rise in stocks over the last year, 2018, if you stayed on the sideline after the last crash, you missed unprecedented growth.

You will recall from the introduction I stated some facts: On October 9, 2007, the Dow Jones Industrial Average hit an all-time high of 14,164. By March 2009, the Dow had fallen over 50 percent to 6,469. How can that be? How can a country that has evolved technologically by leaps and bounds since that time fall once again? Unfortunately, most of us did not ask that question. On June 28, 2013, the Dow Jones Industrial Average, the Dow, was at 14,909. In 2016, the fifty-two-week low was 15,451 with the high being 18,668. On March 25, 2017, the Dow closed at 20,596. When do you buy? When do you sell? Should I panic and sell everything, or will the increase we have been seeing for years now continue? No matter how you look at it however, those were scary times.

On January 2, 2018, the Dow Jones was at 24,824. By February, the Dow had soared over 26,500. However, no one can predict what will happen. Everyone has a different tolerance for risk, and they can change over time. One moment, you may take a chance on a certain investment, while at another moment, you may not. The key is to be in the market over long periods of time. On February 9, 2018, the market sunk quicker than any time in history, losing more than 12 percent in a matter of days with 1,000-plus-point swings to now close the week at 24,190. 2018 has seen many new all-time highs and euphoria, followed by earth shattering declines causing panic and pessimism. As I write this on Christmas Eve, December 24, 2018, panic is once again everywhere with the Nasdaq, S&P 500 in correction territory (a fall of more than 20% from their highs) and the DJIA not too far behind.

What do you do by way of taking advice? It always makes me laugh when I see so-called experts on television making bold promises and predictions. If they turn out to be right, they profess to the world that they are the authorities and how right they were. They then may make predictions that go horribly wrong but blame that on an isolated factor that caused their prediction to go awry.

If you rely on TV experts, you'll have some difficult decisions. You turn on one channel, and the leading expert on gold says that you must buy now, as the opportunity is at an all-time high. You click another station only to find another expert on stocks saying you should place all your money in the stock market and avoid gold, as that would be a mistake. And then a coworker tells you that his brother's girlfriend's uncle is in a car pool with someone who knows the maid of the CEO of XYZ Corporation where she overheard that he would be acquiring a major competitor and you should by that stock.

You're on vacation and by the pool. You strike up a conversation with a gentleman in his fifties. You learn he's retired, travels around the world with his wife, and lives off his investments. Your curiosity is piqued, and you ask him how he managed to quit working way before age sixty-five. He says he began investing at a young age and never read the *Wall Street*

Journal or other business magazines and doesn't watch the financial news or similar sites. He tells you that when he was eighteen, his grandfather gave him the secret of financial success—pay yourself first. He meant investing 10 percent of everything you earn in a well-diversified portfolio consistently even through ups and downs. He says his grandfather handed him a card with a hundred-dollar bill in it and said, "Start today." He listened to his grandfather and never forgot this rule.

At that same pool is a younger, thirty-something woman having a great time with her friends. You find out she's the CEO of a startup she founded with a hundred dollars. Though her idea for her company sounded crazy to others, it took off. Five years later, she was bought out by a larger company for $50 million.

Across the country, a farming family wakes up at four in the morning just as they and their forebears did. They eat breakfast and then work a fifteen-hour day and will do so till they retire, when the next generation will do the same. They earn enough to get by, and their land is worth a lot, but they'll never sell it. They've been conditioned to do as their parents and grandparents had done. Conversations with them as far as what to invest in will be quite different. They'll tell you to work hard and invest in your land, which will provide for you. They are beyond happy and exude the dying art of a strong work ethic.

In school, children are told that the way to succeed is to get a college degree and then a job and work hard; they are told to invest in themselves. Countless highly educated people followed this path toward promised prosperity. Instead of getting the dream job that would provide for them or any job, they find that their investment did not pay off. Instead, they find themselves competing with hundreds of other equally qualified graduates for the same job while they are strapped with extravagant student loans that will come due with interest and throw them further into debt. That's okay, you say, because they have degrees.

Some will find jobs in which they can grow and follow a path to happiness and longevity, and they will be in a culture that will help them learn, grow, and be a part of something bigger than themselves with a compelling future. That, however, is rare.

I'm proud of the culture that we have created at LaMonaca Law that attracts people who share our core values and want careers—not just jobs. I am equally proud of the longevity of our team members; some have been here more than eighteen years. I like to think it's because of my upbringing and my utilizing all the information in this book that allowed me to initially create something special and different. It's now something we as a team share and take pride in being a part of. As my team members will tell you, we don't just run a law practice; instead, we share certain core values that separate us from other businesses. As the leader of the firm, I take the responsibility of teaching, educating, mentoring and contributing all the knowledge in this book to each of my team members so they can in turn teach others.

Many will tell you that education is a waste of time and you should focus on being an entrepreneur, the only way to succeed. The following is a list of individuals who did not finish school:

- Bill Gates and Paul Allen (founders of Microsoft)
- Steve Jobs and Steve Wozniak (founders of Apple)
- Mark Zuckerberg (founder of Facebook)
- Richard Branson (founder of Virgin Atlantic Airways and Virgin Records)
- Andrew Carnegie (industrialist)
- Charles Dickens (author)
- Carly Fiorina (CEO of Hewlett Packard)
- Ted Turner (founder of CNN)
- John D. Rockefeller (founder of Standard Oil)
- Peter Jennings (news anchor for ABC)
- Ray Kroc (founder of McDonald's)
- Benjamin Franklin (US ambassador)
- George Washington (president of the United States)
- Abraham Lincoln (president of the United States)
- Winston Churchill (prime minister of England)

I am not suggesting that you should not pursue advanced education. I certainly did, and it has rewarded me immensely. I bring this to the table

as only another thing to consider when determining whom to listen to and what advice and path to take. As an attorney, I could not have evolved to my status without the valuable degree I received from West Chester University and the law degree I obtained from Widener University School of Law; these fine institutions allowed me to flourish on my chosen path.

My path is but one to consider among many. I may preach, but I also practice what I preach, and that's worked for me. I value higher education, and I value the education you can get after you graduate from any school. This is the time I believe that true education begins. You learn from doing and improving yourself by way of books, seminars, audio programs, podcasts, listening to other experts, and many other ways outside a classroom.

As I mentioned in the introduction, I was taught the basics that have been ingrained in me as far back as I can recall. Show respect to elders, say please and thank you, save money, dollar-cost average, diversify, invest in stocks, invest in real estate, get a good education, be debt free, be ahead of the curve with technology, never stop learning, read and study the greats, mentor others, give back, and work hard. If you do these things, you are almost certain to succeed; they're the basic ingredients of a proven recipe for success. They give you faith and confidence to weather the storms. Those who were able to ride out the storm and continued to buy on the way down as opposed to panic selling were rewarded.

I believe that what is significantly lacking today is a strong work ethic. This staple our country was founded on is slowly eroding to what is now the entitlement mentality many have. This is a belief that others such as the government, your parents, family, and friends can take care of you. Instead of saving, investing, and being personally accountable, they go further into debt while living day to day.

What is one to do when faced with so much contradictory advice? At the core is taking 100 % personal accountability. We all are responsible for our actions. If we choose to go to college, not go to college, start our own company, read books, take seminars, and so on, we must first be firmly committed to the all-important first step. We cannot rely on our parents, neighbors, television gurus, the government, the guy or gal by the pool, or this book for that matter. We certainly can and should take advice from a diversified assortment of reliable sources. In the end, we decide how we will live and what we will do. We rise and fall by our actions; it's not up to our parents or the government to provide for our future. We alone are responsible for choosing the path we take. In that vein, as you read these twenty-five suggestions of mine, use them as but one source for your consideration.

There is no guarantee even if you implement these ideas that you will be successful. You must always be willing to course correct. What works for one individual at a particular moment cannot guarantee similar results for another at another moment. As you study many successful individuals, however, you'll see patterns and clues. My purpose in writing this book is twofold as it pertains to this idea. One is to give you ideas and suggestions to add to your personal repertoire if they fit with your goals and values. The second purpose is quite the opposite. I want you to look at all my advice critically and question whether it can apply to you, whether things have changed, and whether what we once accepted as true is no longer the case. Will the brick truly fall, or will it start floating? The critical first step is to acknowledge that you are ultimately responsible for the decisions you make regarding your whole life, not just your finances and investments.

I've received financial advice at times from very well respected individuals and advisers that lost me thousands. Was I upset? Of course. Did I let that stop me? Of course not. I considered each one of those situations an investment in my knowledge. As you will see, by not putting all my eggs in one basket, I was able to move on.

In a society fueled by a spend-today mentality and instant gratification, we must block out the many sources of temptations. By avoiding unnecessary spending and doing a complete review of all your expenses, I guarantee that you will find additional income to help you on your path to prosperity. I subscribe to the pay-yourself-first mentality; put a percentage of everything you earn into savings before you do anything else with your money. Consider yourself your own creditor who wants a payment every month, and make that creditor the first on your list to pay. By freeing up money in ways I have suggested, you'll be able to do that. Try as hard as you can to stick with the percentage you can handle. Thousands of successful individuals I've studied subscribe to this plan.

I heard about this from one of my earliest mentors, John M. Hickey, Esquire, better known as Wolf. He was an extremely successful attorney and the father of one of my closest friends, Joseph Hickey, Esquire, who along with his two brothers are very successful attorneys. I was fortunate to have rented office space in the same building as Wolf and his firm had, and I found myself as a young and impressionable attorney sitting in his office on many occasions talking about life and the law. Among the many valuable lessons he taught me was this rule of paying yourself first, and he suggested 10 percent. I listened to Wolf; from that day forward, I did just that, and since that day, I've seen firsthand the benefits of this rule.

Now that you freed up additional money and have paid yourself first, your next priority is to set up a safety and security fund, which I covered earlier. Make sure it's enough to support you and your family for at least six months if not a year or more, and make sure it's liquid. That's the money you'll rely on to see you through emergencies, not to pay for a vacation to Maui. Once you do this, you won't worry every day about how you'll handle the what-ifs. And if you ever have to dig into it, make sure you begin to replenish it as soon as you can.

The next step is to set up an automatic investment program so you don't have to even remember to pay yourself first. There are advisers out there who can help you develop a plan suited to you. The key is time. Start today. Every day you wait will put you further behind. It could be as simple as setting up a 401(k) or a self-directed retirement account with your employer that's funded every time you get paid. (More about this in future chapters.) Decide what you can set aside this way based on your present situation and your goals, and make it automatic. I know what you're saying—"I don't need to do that. I'm responsible enough to take the amount out each payday and invest it." Regardless of your good intentions, it will not always work that way. Life's inevitable curveballs will have different plans for you at times. Make it automatic, and do it today!

Once you set up this automatic investment account, you'll start seeing the value of compound interest that Einstein and Warren Buffet professed. When you combine this with the debt-reduction strategies discussed earlier, you can start imagining a time when your debts will be zero and your net worth will be climbing. Without debt, your risk tolerance will increase and you'll save more than 10 percent and perhaps invest in that business you always wanted to start, vacation homes, investment real estate, and so on. Monica and I have followed this path.

Many of you are thinking that this path is contrary to this book's introduction that outlined the economic collapse.

Question: Why would anyone want to invest in stock with the following statistics? On October 9, 2007, the Dow Jones Industrial Average hit an all-time high of 14,164. By March 2009, the Dow had fallen over 50 percent to 6,469.

Answer: On January 4, 2018, the Dow got back to 25,067.

Question: I hear what you're saying, Greg, but just one month later, on February 9, 2018, the market sunk quicker than any time in history and lost more than 12 percent in a matter of days with 1,000-plus-point swings to close the week at 24,190. Why the hell would I invest now?

Answer: Because while no one has a crystal ball to predict the future, history is one of our best guides. Historically, we know that since the beginning of the stock market, we typically get corrections, drops of 10 percent or more from its peak, once a year. We get a bear market, a 20 percent or more drop, once every several years. It is normal for this to occur, and it's healthy. If you know this and prepare for it, you won't panic when the events occur. If you utilize the lessons in this book and prepare proactively, you can create financial abundance for you and your children.

Question: Why would anyone invest in real estate when home prices throughout most of the country plummeted and had an epic collapse a few years back?

Answer: I own my home in West Chester, Pennsylvania, and I own our three law office buildings in Media, Pennsylvania, that I bought during two downturns in the market. Coincidentally, as I write this, the March 2017 cover of *Philadelphia Magazine* is entitled "The Suburbs strike back ... the burbs remake themselves for a new generation." The story begins with the caption "The hottest Suburban towns. The first feature story and town on page 81 is "West Chester, the buzzy borough that only gets better, up 15 percent (Five-year change in home value)." The very next story and town is "Media, New retail, new life for whole country, up 17% (One-year change in home value in Media)."

My belief system is the sum of fifty years of life and thousands of books, seminars, audios, trusted advisers, discussions with my wife, mentors, advisors and life's lessons. The combination has given my wife and me, a team, a belief system. Our knowledge and our plan are based not on one period of time but on the combination of all the above principles, habits, and values that have allowed us to make informed decisions.

My mother decided to stay out of the stock market during the time when the market last crashed and to be in cash. Considering my parents' ages and risk profile, that was the right decision, and it proved to be an amazing decision given the collapse of the stock market. When panic began to set in nationwide, my wife and I of course were not happy to see our paper assets plummet, but instead of panicking, we saw the opportunity of a lifetime because we had already decided what we would do during such a time many years earlier. Not having debt allowed us to go on. We continued to pay ourselves first, invested that, and reinvested our dividends; that allowed us to buy stock in some of the premier companies in the world at bargain-basement prices. We did not sell. We did not panic. Knowing that we had (God willing) many more years in the market, we were able to ride out the economic storm, and when it was all over, our portfolio soared to new heights. This was the psychology mentioned at the outset. By planning and knowing that corrections and recessions will occur, we turned problems into opportunities. By diversifying in our stock portfolio and further diversifying with real estate and other investments, we weren't prone to panic, and we stuck to our proactive plan as opposed to what many others did by reacting—selling in a panic.

We focused on what we could control—reducing our debt, our careers, our team of advisers, a strong work ethic, and a strong belief in all the systems we put in place. Times are good again, but we won't start thinking they will remain that way. As I review this in February 2018, the stock market is at all-time highs due to a bull market that has gone on far longer than the norm, but I know that a correction or a recession could occur.

Through proper planning, when it occurs, you can once again have the opportunity to buy investments at extremely low prices. The key therefore is to develop both a psychology and a proactive system in advance of the next correction or worse. When times are good, that's the time to plan for the next inevitable dip. Learn from the past because it leaves clues. Follow the clues and you will increase your chance for success.

How is this for timing? As I was proofreading this on February 2, 2018, a day after all-time highs, the Dow dropped 666 points, an ominous number on an ominous day. Or was it? Talks of a recession and hikes in interest rates sent the Dow dropping like an anvil. Devastation, doom, and gloom everywhere. Between the time I wrote the paragraph above and was proofing this on the week ending February 9, 2018, the market sunk quicker than any time in history losing more than 12 percent in a matter of days with 1,000-plus-point swings and closed the week 24,190. That week, I bought and bought as each day presented many opportunities to buy great stocks going down with the rest of the market for no apparent reason. Even with these large drops, formally a correction, I didn't put all my money in. No. I was disciplined in my plan, trusted it, and stuck with it. We'll be in for some rocky roads ahead, but fortunes are made during such times of uncertainty.

The market then later reached all-time highs in 2018, only to have it once again plummet into a bear market near the end of the year. Panic setting in, correct? No. For me, this was/is the financial Super Bowl. (Note also the reference as the Philadelphia Eagles, who played in this year's Super Bowl against the New England Patriots, and won! … But I digress.) I had been planning for declines like this for many years. I had sidelined cash for when, not if, such declines would come. I'm not a stock trader, so short-term pullbacks are of no concern to me; I'm in it for the long term. Market corrections and Bear markets are great times to buy great stocks. As the market kept dropping at various times this year, I bought stocks to safely reallocate our portfolio. As most of the world panicked, I have been buying up bargain basement stocks at great prices. It was a great year to load up on stocks across the board as everyone was dumping them. The secret was that I was prepared and had a plan for just such an occasion. While no one can predict the future, and I have no way of knowing how 2019 and beyond will be, I do feel confident that the long historical cycle of ups, downs, corrections, bear markets, will eventually give way to another bull market. It is then, that the seeds I have planted throughout 2018 will flourish.

By way of example, on this Christmas Eve, December 24, 2018, doom and gloom was everywhere, making it the worst Christmas Eve in history. All of the experts were on television giving their "expert" opinions of how we were heading into recession, crashes and many other pieces of wisdom. Well, the very next trading day, December 26, 2018, after the close of the market, the headlines read, "Dow logs biggest daily point gain ever," as it surged 1,086.25 points.

When I purchased the stocks above, I did not put all my cash to work. Instead, I bought a predetermined amount on each dip so that if there were another drop, which there always is, I'd evaluate that dip and see what was on sale.

As they say, no good plan stays that way forever. It is very important to monitor your progress to ensure you're on track or to get back on track. At times, you'll need to change your goals based on life events. Likewise, with time comes additional technology and information that you can review to see if it helps or hurts your plans. The point is to review your plan at least quarterly to ensure you're on track. Equally important is to consult with your partner to make sure his or her goals have not changed and your goals harmonize. In my family law practice at LaMonaca Law, we see daily that when communication, agreement, and harmony are lacking in a marriage, the chance of divorce skyrockets, and finances are one of the leading causes of divorce.

Develop a plan that best serves your needs. Have fun learning and growing together, and take full accountability for your and your family's future. Research, read, and find the information you need from several well-respected sources. Get a plan that best suits you and your families long term goals. Close the television, put down the paper, avoid the so called experts, and stick to your plan with a good, overall allocation of investments. The more you take accountability for your education, the better you'll be able to make the decisions necessary for your family. As they say, the future is yours, so what will you do about it?

8. Save for Retirement

I attended a retirement party for my father many years ago in South Philadelphia. Friends, family, and colleagues gathered for lunch and to hear some nice speeches about my father—his dedication, loyalty, and long-standing work ethic. He worked for decades for the government in the Defense Personnel Support Center. He got up early, drove to work each day, and returned promptly to have dinner with my mom and his children each night. He received a watch that day, but he also started receiving a lifetime pension.

The type of pension my parents enjoy is often called a defined-benefit pension; it provides for retirees indefinitely, but such pensions are few and far between these days as I've discovered in my law practice. They've been phased out by most every company. That means that many people who had not planned for retirement have had to go back to work.

Today, with the demise of these traditional pensions that took care of you for life, employees need to take care of themselves if they work for an employer that even offers plans. Replacing the older defined-benefit pensions are the newer defined-contribution plans such as 401(k)s, 403(b)s, and other plans with confusing numbers and letters. While these plans have great potential and often find employers matching a percentage of what the employees invest, it requires the employees to elect to save as opposed to making it mandatory as it was with the older pensions.

Many young workers today elect to spend the extra twenty-five or fifty dollars on immediate pleasures instead of investing it for their future, which they think is too far off to worry about. They keep saying, "I'll start investing someday," but months and years pass and they're still talking about someday. Their future is bleak; many of them will retire without any savings and possibly without Social Security, and they'll leave their care in the hands of the government assuming it can afford to take care of them.

We must educate our youth about retirement and the importance of beginning investing now to make sure they take advantage of employer plans and other forms of retirement savings. Even a small weekly savings amount will add up over the years, but they say, "Does it really matter? I can always save later after I have a little fun. I know what I'm doing. Other people have that problem, not me. I'm smarter." We never think things we read about will happen to us. We think we're smarter than others, and we have a plan that is different.

People come to me in crisis in the wake of a divorce or custody dispute. They may have been living very comfortable lives keeping up with the Joneses, buying pricy cars and big homes, taking fancy vacations, and going on spending sprees. Now, when they are confronted with a divorce, their futures they thought would be filled with travel, relaxation, and the finer things in life look bleak. They wonder how they'll be able to pay back all the debt while supporting their children and a new residence.

Successful marriages are partnerships of two individuals who complement each other with different skills that add value to their marriages and combined create dynamic units. What I see with many of my clients is that one is usually in charge of handling the bills and investments while the other handles other family matters. When you have a healthy, thriving, lifelong marriage, that is outstanding. When, however, the marriage dissolves and the spouses go their separate ways, the spouse with the lack of financial knowledge can be devastated. It's sad when I review my clients' financial profiles and have to tell them they don't have a retirement plan, they have an inadequate plan, their spouses may have taken out loans against the plan, or liquidated it and incurred significant penalties and lost interest, or any one of countless other horrific situations.

I also find cases where despite the two individuals' inability to have a healthy and thriving marriage, they nonetheless did save for retirement. When I am representing the dependent spouses who have not been involved with dealing with these plans, I am comforted that I can tell them while their marriages may be dissolving, their and their children's financial futures are secure.

You don't have to be in a divorce situation to find this scenario. When I meet new clients, I go through a comprehensive screening and evaluation of all areas of their lives. My goal is to determine what they have been doing well and where they might need assistance and guidance.

By identifying these gaps, I can begin helping them fill them in and create new, dynamic, and empowered individuals as they begin the next chapters of their lives; I get the pleasure of witnessing amazing transformations from fear to empowerment as they regain control of their lives.

By performing this financial audit, I can provide them immediate and direct information that can assist them. It may be simple advice—a referral to a course or a book. If there are gaps in their knowledge of finances, I refer them to other professionals, perhaps a CPA, a financial planner, a mortgage broker, and others who can delve in deeper and help our clients come up with detailed and personalized plans. Our clients end up understanding their financial situations and know what steps to take to address their future retirement needs. Notice I wrote "their" future retirement needs. This is at the core of Brutally Honest, which does not say, "Do as I have done" but says, "Let's come up with a plan based on your unique requirements and needs that will best suit you."

These rules apply to everyone, not just those going through divorce. Those in happy, lifelong marriages have an equal need to know what is going on with their retirement. We are all obliged to gain at least a minimum amount of knowledge about our retirement options and to play an active part in knowing what is going on.

When it comes to retirement or anything having to do with finances, rule number one is, "Be an active participant." Regardless of your expertise or involvement in monthly bill paying, investment decisions, and so on, you must participate. Monica is my best friend, my soul mate; our marriage is a true partnership in which we bring our separate and distinct knowledge to the marriage that combines to make up a dynamic and thriving family unit. We have disagreements and arguments, but we work things out and overcome obstacles, break through barriers, and take our marriage to the next level. More important, I've learned the importance of two words: "Yes, dear." lol.

A key difference between what Monica and I have compared with what many of the clients I represent have is a process. We do not assume a great marriage is defined by never disagreeing. If that's your standard, you have set yourself up for failure. A marriage is not a dictatorship; it's two individuals bringing to the marriage unique, wonderful identities that combined create an unbreakable bond. This type of marriage will experience disagreements, obstacles, unexpected events, and countless other issues, but it will have in place ways of addressing these inevitable scenarios not if but when they occur. Open, honest, frequent discussions ensure that these scenarios will be addressed and turned into positive life lessons that solidify a marriage or any other relationship.

Monica and I have different and distinct roles as it pertains to our finances, investments, and retirement planning. We utilize our separate skills to add to our family unit. We discuss these things throughout the month as things evolve, we have specific meetings in the home where we sit down to review the many different areas, we have dinners during which we discuss certain planning, and we meet many times throughout the year with our trusted accountant, financial advisers, and others. Before you say, "Great for you!" let me say that we couldn't even pay our bills let alone hire accountants and financial planners if we hadn't already covered the basics.

Before I started to practice law, before Monica and I started planning our future, mentors taught me to take personal responsibility for my financial future much as I am teaching you now. I read books, listened to audio seminars, and attended many seminars that have played significant roles in where we are today. As I learned each additional fact, I shared it with Monica. She also read many of the books I did, and we discussed their contents. I listened to Tony Robbins's *Unshakeable—Your Financial Freedom Playbook* as I drove to work. Monica listened to CDs, and she shared what she had learned, and we discussed particular topics as they pertained to us. As I told that member of my law firm that I had not simply come up with my knowledge on so many topics, Monica and I did not just arrive with the knowledge we have; it was the result of decades of our combined learning and planning.

In my vast personal library, about fifty books hold a particular spot of honor on one shelf; they are the books that have most influenced me at some period of my life. They may not be the best books of all time, they may contain things I don't necessarily believe in, and their information may be outdated, but I'd read each one at a time when it resonated with me, impacted me, transformed me, and fueled some amazing change.

One of these books, *The 9 Steps to Financial Freedom* by Suze Orman, is one such book. As I mentioned earlier, Monica and I read it together early on in our marriage, implemented the lessons in that book, and had fun working together to achieve each milestone. Today, as we take trips as a family, we play empowering audio books in the car and discuss them. We play board games that teach or reinforce financial literacy. We grow as a family and support each other.

Today, you have few excuses for not accessing an easily accessible, unlimited supply of free information. Google financial literacy, retirement planning, or any other search terms that define the areas in which you want more knowledge; the information is free, immediate, and plentiful. Beyond that, ask others who have been where you want to go. Ask questions of family, friends, and advisers. Be careful, however, to ask only those who are successful in what you want to do. Many will profess to know what they are doing and want to sell you things when they themselves have not done so.

Commit today to sitting down in the next few days and writing out a plan to address any of your financial fears. Be Brutally Honest with yourself. By identifying the areas that make you fearful, you can then put together a plan to address each one. If you can, sit down with a qualified financial planner or accountant to review your current situation and develop a retirement plan that best fits your risk tolerance and goals.

The better advisers not only advise you about what's best for you; they also educate you about each alternative so you can actively participate in making the right decisions. It's their job to educate and advise you, give you your options and their pros and cons, and make recommendations. If you've done your own research as well, you'll be able to understand the advice and options and make the best choices for you and your family. Monica and I seek out advice from our adviser and follow it, but at times, we've taken a different path based on our understanding all our options.

I've given you a snapshot of our lives and how we've done things. Let me assure you that notwithstanding our planning, we have made mistakes and bad investments and have lived through several market corrections and recessions. Our finances have been smacked back and forth quicker than a tennis ball at a championship match. But as I mentioned, we learned from each mistake, and we are prepared to weather the next storm.

As I write this in early 2018, the economy has been on a multiyear upswing after coming through a horrific period. The market soared after President Trump won the election. That said, it did the same thing with former presidents with the ups coming with any news of optimism only to fall on news of pessimism.

It is easy to jump on the bandwagon of the television pundits who are patting themselves on the back, exalting their outstanding accomplishments, and preaching about how their method is the best. Turn the channel and there is another expert saying the exact opposite. The bottom line is that the economy will turn down again, so now's the time to prepare for that—work with your adviser and get ahead of the curve. Act today to ensure you will be financially sound come retirement. Acknowledge that you alone are responsible for taking the appropriate steps to educate yourself about your current situation and your options for securing your retirement. Determine whom you can add to your personal financial team to educate and advise you and to increase the likelihood that your future will be bright and your retirement years will be rewarding. If you are in a committed relationship, work together to create a dynamic team consisting of complementary skills. If you have children, involve them in age-appropriate lessons and games they can learn from while having fun. Learn together, grow together, and have fun in the process.

What plans will you start making today to secure your family's retirement?

9. Stay Positive

My family, clients, and friends have heard my mantra a thousand times: "Focus on what you can control as opposed to what you cannot." During economic turmoil, or any of life's unexpected surprises, it's easy to lose faith and become stressed. Likewise, when life deals you a pleasant surprise, it's easy to feel elated. I've been through every conceivable emotion. Fear comes from the unknown. We go through life trying to understand what is happening and what lies ahead. When we focus on the unknown and go through the what-ifs, we can drive ourselves crazy.

We simply cannot predict the future, where life will take us, when we will leave this earth, where the economy will be next year or in five or twenty years. It's easy to get caught up in this endless loop of worry. Take a moment to think about your past, times when you were faced with something that worried you. Where were you then? How old were you? What fear did you envision? Make it real in your head. You probably wrestled with all the possible reasons your fears would come true and the worst-case scenario would occur. Once you start down that slippery slope, your mind takes over and creates more fears and concerns. While some amazing writers can create masterpieces that allow us to escape into various adventures, there is no greater writer than the brain; it can create love stories, horror stories, action-adventure masterpieces, and a limitless assortment of infinite endings. If you begin your story with all the negative things that could happen, your brain will take over and create the world's greatest tragedy ... if you let it.

How many of your fearful times ended up with the negative consequences you had envisioned? If you're like most people, your answer is, "Not many." Most of the stress and anxiety we let ourselves go through turns out to be unnecessary. Imagine recapturing all that negative energy, anxiety, and worry and replacing it with positive, uplifting thoughts and events. An hour of worry replaced by an hour of playing catch with your children, taking a walk with your spouse or significant other, writing a letter to or calling a friend, starting to write that book you've always wanted to write, reading a book, or something else positive.

Okay, enough doom and gloom. After all, this chapter is entitled "Staying Positive." While that same supercomputer we call our brain has the power to create futuristic negative events, it also has the power to create powerful, positive, and compelling outcomes and thoughts. By engaging in conscious, focused, and positive thoughts, we start eliminating self-doubt and negativity and start creating empowering thoughts that give us momentum and tilt our internal pendulums from the negative side to neutral and finally to the positive side. This process involves positive visualizations combined with invoking all our senses.

I don't want to infer that if we do this, we will avoid all of life's unpleasantness. If the stock market is going to crash, that will happen whether we are positive or not. Here's some more breaking news—at some point, hopefully light-years from now, you'll die as will all of those you love. You'll get sick at times, break things, have your feelings hurt, be taken advantage of by people you trust, and experience thousands of other negative events. They will occur. Are you amazed at this earth-shattering news? Of course not. My point is that you should not wait around for these inevitable events to occur.

In my book *The Brutally Honest Pennsylvania Divorce & Custody Survival Guide*, (released in late 2013 and revised in 2018 and available for free as a download on the LaMonaca Law website at www.lamonacalaw.com, I discuss a technology I created and called VAKOG.

> In December of 2012, I purchased the four-thousand-square-foot historic Appleton Building. The building was completely renovated from top to bottom to make real my vision. The building now incorporates the technological system I created, which is referred to as VAKOG Technology. VAKOG is an acronym for all the senses:
>
> **V** = Visual (What we see)
>
> **A** = Auditory (What we hear)

K = Kinesthetic (What we feel)*

O = Olfactory (What we smell)*

G = Gustatory (What we taste)*

*Note: While these particular senses have literal meanings, in the present context, they may also connote a feeling one gets, a sense or perception. For example, one may say, "I have a good feeling about something." This would fall under Kinesthetic. One might say, "This doesn't smell right to me." This would fall under Olfactory. One may say, "I have a bad taste in my mouth about this situation." This would fall under Gustatory.

At its core, this system stands for the premise that, by invoking each additional sense, one increases his or her ability, both to perceive an incoming message or recognize a situation observed, and to convey an outgoing message, and to communicate about a situation. As a part of this system, I utilize video enhancement technology to work with our clients to help get them to their goals. The building was equipped with state of the art video equipment, audio devices, Skype technology, Amazon Alexa throughout and more, to allow us to interact with clients, or other experts and professionals from all over the world. I have a big screen television on the wall in my office, which was built to accommodate this interaction with the client, and we have space for a fully functioning film studio. Using this equipment, combined with VAKOG technology, our clients can observe the various triggers that may cause them to show increased anxiety, as well as the triggers that make them happy. Clients learn to identify and replicate negative stimuli, by way of seeing exactly what impression they are giving to the rest of the world. Using this technology helps clients to break through barriers, both emotionally and physically, and allows them to see and focus on what may be holding them back.

VAKOG has proven to be a powerful tool in my practice and my life. Most people don't realize what they're giving off to the world. Did you ever have someone say, "You don't look well. Are you okay?" You say, "I'm fine" and have no idea what that person was talking about. Your body gives off thousands of simultaneous signals others can take note of. To one, a smile denotes happiness, but to another, it denotes smugness.

In the beginning of this chapter, I had you recall an event that had caused you to worry unnecessarily. Now, I want you to think of one of your goals for next year. If you follow my suggestions in this book and in *The Brutally Honest Life Management Journal* 2009, you will already have written goals in your journal. Pick one. Close your eyes and get a picture of what this goal will look like when you achieve it. How does it feel? Sound? Look like? Imagine these things combining and creating a compelling, realistic feeling in your mind as if it has already occurred.

Your mind cannot distinguish between fiction and reality. Augmented reality and virtual reality are based on this phenomenon. In the near future, we will place headsets on that will allow us to conduct virtual meetings with people across the country but in a virtual room that makes us think we are all together.

By consciously focusing on positive outcomes, by creating a virtual positive world in your mind, you are creating signals and a mental road map to get you to that outcome. If you leave your mind to its own devices, it will easily and often slip back to creating negative outcomes. The key word in this paragraph is *consciously*. I wrote this chapter to help you shift your pendulum to the positive side. By consciously focusing on positive outcomes, you are controlling this. You'll get what you focus on, and focusing on positive outcomes will create an avalanche of positive events in many areas of your and your loved ones' lives.

Staying positive is perhaps the single greatest way to help you focus, overcome adversity, and move in the right direction. When you face a negative situation or thought, ask yourself, *What else could this mean? How can I benefit from the situation?* When the economy sank, it took with it many great companies. But if you continued to dollar-cost average into these stocks or bought them on a decline, when they came back (assuming they did), you would have bought the shares at bargain-basement prices. If you bought a home in that environment, you would have most likely purchased it at a record low with an equally low mortgage. If you waited, mortgages continued to break record after record. The stock market came back in a big way. It's all about focus and perspective. It doesn't mean that you'll always be right, but since you cannot do anything about the actual outcome—whether the stock or housing market will rebound or dissolve—why live in misery and assume only the negative? Keep focused on the positive while being prepared for potential negative outcomes; just don't live in misery, doom, and gloom. One clue that you are doing this is when friends or family members tell you about a problem they have. Do you listen and support their feelings, or do you tell them how bad you're doing?

What positive opportunities can you create out of an otherwise negative situation, event, or occurrence? Using all the senses of VAKOG, describe how your number-one goal will be when you accomplish it. Commit today to plan for the worst-case scenario while living in the positive, wonderful, and present world. Ask yourself, *What am I most grateful for?*

10. Create a Compelling Vision

What does it mean to have a compelling vision? To compel is to force or drive something. Within each of us lies a driving force that guides us through each day. That special part of us gets us up in the morning when we would otherwise want to sleep in. As I proofread this section in 2018, I plan to later go downstairs and engage in day four of a weekly series of weight workouts. Without fail, every week, I break the body down in half. Day one (Tuesday), I do back, biceps, traps and legs. On day two, it's chest, shoulders, and triceps. I repeat this two-day series again every Saturday and Sunday. I do stomach every day and cardio at least four to five days as well. I have been training in various forms of martial arts, and martial arts weapons for years. They complement my weekly workouts. That's been my regimen in some form or another for decades. From time to time, for variety, I'll work in some specialty programs typically with Monica.

I originally documented one of these specialty programs a few years back this way.

I am completing week seven of an intense morning workout called P90x3. This is an intense workout that takes thirty minutes to do each morning. Having done the original version a couple of times years back called P90x, as well as P90x2 years later, where the daily workouts took anywhere from one to one and a half hours, this newest version is designed to be done quicker. With the quickness however comes increased intensity to get the same effects. I am doing this workout with Monica, the same way that we did the first version together. I am naturally a morning person. Monica, not so much!

> To do this work out, like the last time, and despite our different internal clocks, we decided to get up early and do it first thing. Initially it was very difficult, even for me. Clearly if all things were equal I would stay in bed till 8 or 9 and get the extra sleep. Things aren't equal however. As has been the case throughout my life, with this year being no different, health and exercise are one of my top priorities. As such, while sleep is also precious, exercise

trumps it. Initially getting up earlier was difficult. My alarm goes off at 4:15 am. I get up, write in my daily journal and gently, and I do mean gently (skills learned through being with her for 36 years) wake Monica. I go down, feed and take care of the dogs, and then head to the basement. I put the days DVD in the machine and get it ready. Monica comes down shortly thereafter and we begin the program. Once done, we are awake, alert and fully energized with that euphoric feeling you get after a satisfying workout. "Our," and I reiterate "our" compelling vision in this regard is to maintain a healthy, fully functioning mind and body. By exercising and cheering on each other we further solidify our relationship, support each other and demonstrate to our children healthy habits. Now, into week 7 of the 12-week program this routine is engrained in us. We simply go to bed earlier where possible to recapture some of the sleep.

Whether it is in the above example as we completed together P90x3 or its predecessors P90x1 and P90x2, any one of the many other routines, or simply as today, a generic weight workout followed by cardio, inherent in each is the drive to always make health and fitness musts in our lives.

What is this drive that motivates us to achieve our goals? Is it innate or learned? I think it's a combination. We are given certain gifts in life while others are learned or better yet earned. We all can better ourselves and our circumstances.

Physiologically, part of the drive that creates our compelling vision is chemical.

- Endorphins lessen the pain within us temporarily. They serve to mask pain with pleasure. Endorphins give Monica and me a euphoric feeling after and during each workout.
- Dopamine creates instant gratification, pushes us, and rewards goal achieving. This chemical gives Monica and me that good feeling that gets us out of bed each morning, makes us feel good

as we progress in our exercise program, and gives us a sense of satisfaction after we achieve our goals. Dopamine is responsible for our immediately checking our phones when we feel the buzz or constantly checking our social-media sites to see what's new.

- Serotonin gives us a feeling of pride as we achieve milestones. It's released when we feel others' respect and feel connected to them. When we achieve a reward recognizing us for something, the serotonin released gives us the sense of pride that goes along with the accomplishment. If we achieve a goal as a team, others on the team also get this release of serotonin as the bond is reinforced.

- Oxytocin forges lasting friendship, love, and trust. Oxytocin is released when Monica and I high-five each other during workouts and hug each other after they're over. Oxytocin is highest in loving relationships in which we voluntarily become vulnerable as the trust deepens.

- Cortisol is responsible for our fight-or-flight response when we feel stressed or sense danger. Cortisol releases adrenaline to prepare the body to deal with a perceived risk. When you watch a horror film and something jumps out, your heart rate jumps as a result of cortisol being released and flooding your body with adrenaline. While cortisol can help us in the short term, having too much for too long can be dangerous.

If life were a book or a computer program, as we are designing our compelling vision, we would program the times and duration of each of the above chemicals to ensure we attain our goals and realize our vision. However, life is not that way, and we should be glad for that. The unpredictability and uncertainty in life makes things interesting.

The interesting part about these chemicals is that our minds do not differentiate between what is real and what is simply in our heads. This allows us to create compelling visions in our heads first. We can use creative visualization to design and replicate the good feelings that release the positive chemicals. If I asked you to describe what your life will look like ten years from now, could you answer me? Do you have a clear, compelling vision of what you're most ideal life looks like? In step two of the Brutally Honest process (in *The Brutally Honest Life Management Journal*), after arriving at souls core in step one, the breakdown phase, you create statement about what your most ideal life would look like ten years in the future. Once you gain clarity through a series of self-directed exercises, step three begins; you begin the journey to attaining your target zones. It all starts with having a clear and compelling vision.

Once you can clearly see yourself attaining your goals in the future, you'll have a stationary target to aim at. All successful leaders have this type of vision. To begin putting the pieces together from this rocky and uncertain economy, from a troubled marriage, health scares, or any other issues you have, having a clear and compelling vision of success ten years out will help you monitor your life each day, calm your fears, and stay focused on your compelling future.

In the original book, we guided the reader through the activity by having them actually see themselves in that moment, hear what is going on, feel the moment, smell what their environment holds, and get a taste of what it's like in the present tense. This is what I created and described in my second book, *The Brutally Honest Pennsylvania Divorce and Custody Survival Guide* 2013 (revised in 2018; free downloadable copy available at www.lamonacalaw.com). This technology called VAKOG (see chapter on "Staying Positive" above) stands for all the senses described. By invoking this technology while creating your compelling vision, you will actually utilize these chemicals in a controlled manner to help you define, design, and visualize your compelling future.

When we wake up in a cold sweat from a scary dream with our hearts pumping, the chemicals mentioned above are released to help our bodies prepare for what our minds have created. After waking up and realizing it was just a dream, we slowly start to come back down to earth, our heart rate lowers, our level of adrenaline lessens, and we feel better. Much like our mind reacts this way during a dream, by partaking in periodic, deliberate, creative, and empowering mental journeys, we will be well on our way toward our compelling future. Before I took part in countless real adventures in life, I took each journey in my mind first.

What does your most ideal life look like ten years in the future? Take a few minutes, invoke all your senses, and describe in vivid detail what you see.

11. What's Going Right?

No, that's not a misprint. It does ask, "What's going right?" not "What's going wrong?" Unfortunately, most people spend their time telling everyone what's going wrong.

Do you find yourself always looking for what's going wrong? Do you look for the worst in your family, friends, coworkers, acquaintances, and the economy? The law of attraction states that you get what you focus on. If all you're looking for is what's going wrong, you'll get it and limit yourself to seeing only these negative attributes. I bet I have your attention and focus on this topic. Now that you're a captive audience, I have an assignment for you. I want you to take an inventory in the next twenty-four hours of all the things you see or hear others talking about. Listen intently as to how they are saying it and what perspectives they have. Whether it is talk shows, the news, or your favorite reality show, determine what they speak about more—what's going right in the world or what's going wrong. I bet that the negatives far outweigh the positives.

I listened to a podcast in which author Tim Ferris was interviewing someone who mentioned a version of this. She had heard that one of the most used phrases is "Woe is me." She said most people could instantly speak or write about what was bothering them but struggled to do the same thing about what was going well.

I cannot tell you the last time I watched a full news show. I must think really hard to remember watching even a partial show. A few years ago, with the exception of the Wall Street Journal, I stopped receiving the daily newspaper. I purposely insulated myself from all the terrible things happening in the world. That's because I want to choose what I feed my mind. If I have a choice between watching news devoted to all the horrific things occurring in the world or spending that same time talking with my family, exercising, reading a book, or listening to an audiobook or podcast about an uplifting topic, I'll always choose the latter. I feed my mind throughout the day with nourishing things that will take me further toward my goals. Living by the belief of constant and never-ending improvement, I bathe my mind with continuous, additional, uplifting, and motivating things each day.

As I mentioned earlier, at the core of my belief system is the idea that there are things we can control and things we cannot. What we have absolute control over is what we focus on. This can be tricky as life gets busy and our minds go on autopilot.

As you go through your day, your mind is processing billions of bits of data in an amazing sequence and system—where you are, what that means, how you feel, flowing blood throughout your body, breathing, moving, and thinking are amazing processes that work without much conscious thought. While this may seem random, much of what is going on is due to the programming you have done throughout your life. Your life experiences and how you have processed and interpreted them all go into your current understanding.

I find that most of the world simply goes through the motions each day. They awake, get coffee, get dressed, and go to work, come home, watch TV, go to bed, and repeat the cycle much as the repeat option on your iPod will start the same playlist over. What we add to our daily playlists will define our lives. If we watch the daily news, we are subjecting ourselves to what the broadcasters decide we should hear, and doom and gloom keeps their audience's attention. While the news contains current events and some happy and uplifting stories, I bet they are in the minority of what's broadcast.

I'm not opposed to anyone's watching the news. Our minds, the most sophisticated computers ever, get data from what we program into it. After exercising in the morning and while making breakfast, I listen to Amazon Echo's five-minute summary of the world's current events (try it by asking Alexa, "Flash Briefing"). So what then do I feed my mind with? Throughout the night, as I awake often, I play uplifting and motivating podcasts. Driving to the office each morning, I listen to audio books that I choose. Because of this planning, I decide what I put into my brain. We are the sum of our life experiences, and we can't control all our experiences, but by eliminating the vast amount of the doom and gloom news, have we suffered? Not even slightly. After selectively and intentionally removing this information from my life years back, I have not suffered; I have thrived. I also have friends, clients, and family members who send me information they think I'd like to have, which keeps me up to speed.

By planning life rather than letting life plan me, I can spend much more of my day focusing on what is going right instead of on what is going wrong. Based on my legal experience, I say that there is a strong correlation between the high rate of divorce and what married couples choose to engage in. We can choose where most of our focus goes, so it stands to reason that in healthy marriages, a focus on trust, communication, teamwork, financial literacy, positive parenting, intimacy, and unconditional love dominates the relationships. Contrarily, in the clear majority of my divorce cases, negativity, nitpicking, and trivial matters dominate. Instead of complimenting and uplifting their spouses, some people criticize, insult, and belittle them.

I've read thousands of pages of the personal journals I have my clients write that cover their relationships with their spouses from the start to the current day. These journals, typically between ten and seventy-five pages, allow me to get many levels below the surface to not only understand what happened but also discover why it happened. Based on all these journals, I have a good idea of what works and what doesn't. At the start, the journals speak of the love, trust, spontaneity, passion, and fun that initially attracted the two to each other. But then I read about the tipping point that began the downward spiral toward distrust, lack of passion, daily criticism, and the many other things that lead to divorce.

Little things that once were discounted or liked turn into annoying things that are no longer accepted. Focusing on what's not going right widens the gap in the relationship. These journals tell me what triggers this downward spiral. My initial focus when meeting new clients is to see if there is a way they can mend their relationships; I'm a strong advocate of marriage or individual counseling. Often, the right therapist or counselor can salvage many of these cases by getting the parties to refocus on the times when things were going right and why. If they can extract the ingredients that made up those great times when their marriages were working well, that can often allow them to use those same ingredients to rekindle, reconnect, and refocus on what's going right currently.

Spouses in crisis often have the potential to create outstanding marriages. Focusing on their problems for weeks, months, and years will lead to trouble. In even the worst cases, there are always things going right that if focused on can change the relationship. I'm not suggesting there's a magic wand that will make all problems disappear. In cases involving infidelity, abuse, lies, and addictions for instance, there can be pain and suffering that may not be able to be mended. Having practiced in this area for decades, I have learned to never judge an individual. I often get calls from well-intentioned relatives of my clients who are not at a loss for reasons the other spouse is the cause of the breakup; they offer some choice words about them and what they would like to see happen. I am happy to have as much information as I can and weigh this into my overall assessment. What I know for sure, however, is that the actual cause in the breakdown of a marriage is rarely the fault of just one. While one may be more culpable than the other, the result is the same. What I also know is that in every case, there was a critical tipping point, that if both had done something different, they could have avoided a broken marriage.

While we can't go back in time, we can move forward with a different perspective. This new perspective, whether gained through counseling or renewed focus, can often be the difference between those who divorce and those who reconcile. In cases of divorce, a renewed focus on what's going right can help both parties heal and move forward in their separate lives. When children are involved, both parties put their differences aside and agree to co-parent for the best interest of their children and help them thrive.

You can control your focus, and with a little effort, you can gain control over your thoughts and take control of your life. What could you see if you consciously looked at what is working right in your life? What positive things are occurring right now? Even if there is a whole list of things someone is doing wrong, by consciously trying to focus on the positive attributes, you can begin to see things in a different way. From this perspective, you can often play a role in changing the negative attributes as well. If you constantly yell, scream, or belittle someone, that will provoke certain outcomes. If, however, you praise, thank, and encourage that same person, chances are the outcome will be radically different. Try complimenting the person and see what happens. Magic can often occur.

Whom in your life can you try a different approach with? How can you go about doing it today?

12. Develop Healthy Habits, Routines, and Rituals

What we do consistently over time will tend to replicate itself. Our habits, routines, or rituals are unique to us. Our goal is to identify things we can do that will improve the quality of our and our families', friends', and team members' lives. This can be a slippery slope as what one individual may define as a healthy habit may be one others avoid.

I have written about many of my habits and rituals that constitute the cornerstone of my beliefs and core values. These habits have become my GPS system that allows me to stay on track during positive and negative times.

Look back over the last year of your life. Try to identify things you have done consistently. Draw a line down the middle of a piece of paper. At the top, write "Past." On one side, write "Positive," and on the other, write "Negative." This simple exercise will allow you to quickly evaluate your habits, routines, and rituals and put them in one column or the other. Then, share the list with your family and close friends to find out if they have anything to add to your list and whether they think your items are in the right column. They might consider something you listed as a positive to actually be a negative. It's all about perspective. You might also find out things you didn't realize you were doing.

In a healthy, thriving relationship, what you believe is positive is just one part of the equation. You might consider golfing a great way to spend time with friends and clients—a good habit as it gives you joy, develops business contacts, and adds value to your life. If, however, you golf several times a week and most weekends, that takes away from quality family time, and your spouse or children might consider your golfing a definite negative. The key is to engage in this exercise with your family to discover their perspectives and make changes to strike a happy, healthy balance.

At the top of another page, write "Forward." After carefully looking at your "Past" sheet, determine which of these positive habits you want to continue but only after answering these questions: How will following these things improve the quality of my and my family's lives? How will I feel after I complete each positive daily task? Does it advance me toward my goals? Does it inspire me? Is it healthy? Is it practical?

As far as the "Negative" side is concerned, write down several reasons each one is a must for you to eliminate moving forward. How will changing these things improve the quality of your life and your families? How will you feel about yourself when you eliminate a negative habit?

As with many of the things we have discussed, a central and powerful action that will increase exponentially your chances of success is writing down and analyzing your thoughts. Simply saying that you will create a positive habit or eliminate a negative one will not get you very far. As I write this chapter, it is New Year's Eve. As I stated in the beginning of this book, when the ball drops on Times Square, millions of people will raise glasses, toast family and friends, and vow to make changes in the new year. How many of these goals will actually come through? Statistically, not many.

I just downloaded a goal app by one of the world's greatest self-help authorities, Brian Tracy. I began listening to Brian's audio seminars over twenty-five years ago. His courses on setting goals, time management, and overall self-improvement are legendary and have formed an important part of my core values. The first part of his new app is a video on setting goals. It begins by Brian asking, "Do you know that only 3 percent of individuals have clear, written, measurable, and time-bound goals? Did you also know that these 3 percent achieve ten times more than those who do not?" That is compelling.

By actively completing the activities in this book, you are entering this elite minority. By planning your life and not allowing life to plan you, by taking time to analyze your life in writing, you will increase your chances of success exponentially.

I have had countless client's complete similar exercises to determine what negative habits and rituals contributed to the problems in their marriages. By taking control of their lives and analyzing the past in writing, they are better able to see the cause and effect and are in a better position to plan their futures and avoiding the pitfalls that have caused them problems in the past and increase the chances of creating compelling futures full of abundance, happiness, and everything they deserve.

There is a direct correlation between the success I have achieved and the degree to which I have implemented and followed positive daily habits. The secret is not just to follow what I or others have done but to identify the habits you can add to your daily agenda that will increase the chances of your achieving your goals.

So when I use the format suggested above and review my past habits and compare them to my current, what I find is that my core habits are the same. Your core habits are what form the chapter headings of your life. Like a book, there are chapters. Within each chapter is the actual content. In life, we tend to keep the positive chapters while eliminating the negative. To that end, the following are excerpts from my personal journals that describes the habits I followed at the time.

> January 31, 2014: Today, I got up early (4:25 a.m.), woke Monica up and went down, took care of the dogs and got the video for P90x3 ready. We did the program, I showered and went to BNI. Today was my time to speak. As usual I did my best to give a passionate, high energy speech. My theme this morning was "Rituals." I told them about the Pocono Summit and my daily rituals that I believe are so important. Rituals, or also "habits" can be ground breaking things that create a positive environment and change the world. Contrarily, bad habits can have the opposite effect. Habits habitually (no pun intended) take twenty days to form.

> While these rituals change, here is what I am currently doing:

> Get up around 1 am (I can't sleep more than a few hours) and I read and check emails, often responding back to clients throughout the night to address their fears and concerns so hopefully they can sleep better;

> Back to bed hitting the satellite radio, tonight I choose Howard Stern, which goes off in an hour. I drift back to sleep;

Get up at 3 a.m., check and respond to client emails and then back to bed, hit radio back on;

At 4:27 the alarm goes off to the iPod with Adelle playing. I am usually automatically up around 4:15 as my body is conditioned for this;

I get out of bed, read the day's daily inspiration in the John Maxwell book Monica gave me. Each day of the year is one lesson followed by lines where he asks a question related to the lesson where I write in the answer. I look at my emails again and respond to more client emails and social media;

I wake Monica and head downstairs. I give the dogs their food and take them out. I take three sips of sugar free red bull. I come back in and head downstairs to set up the days P90X3 DVD. I begin stretching through the intense pain of my newly constructed body made up of removed bones, inserted metal, misalignment, multiple scars, adhesions and a plethora of life's reminders. It would be so much easier to stay in bed and sleep and use the excuse about all of the abovementioned deterrents but that simply is not me. Complaining and making excuses is not in my DNA. Problems are just obstacles seeking solutions. Monica comes down with that tired face. I am as proud of her as she has been there each day. She is not a morning person, but she is committed to improving and exercising with me. We then beat the hell out of our bodies as we complete that day's video. I note that Monica and I have repeated this routine year after year with the original P90x done several years, P90x2 and now 3.

After the workout, with sweat dripping and heart pumping. We head upstairs.

I make a bowl of oatmeal while looking at emails on my iPad. Specifically, I play the "Minute with Maxwell" daily one minute word of the day. I then read Seth Godin's blogs. I answer client emails. I send out an inspirational Facebook post on the LaMonaca Law Facebook page. I may post some Pinterest pictures, add something to twitter or linked in. Keep in mind that this all takes place as I am eating my oatmeal.

I get my vitamins out and Liss'. I get the green fruit drink out of the frig. I get a silver martini shaker. I fill up a third with the cold, green fruit drink, a third of water and a scoop of green powder. I mix it and drink it while taking my vitamins, fish oil and a probiotic. I then wash out the shaker and fill half with the cold green fruit drink, half apple juice (or other fruit juice) and a scoop of the green powder. I mix it and put it on the table for Liss next to the vitamins. I then get rice checks from the cabinet. The dogs instantly rise and meet me at the table. I take sixteen rice chex perfectly arranged in pairs with three on the top (yes, I know your thinking ocd, and you would be right. lol). I leave these for Liss to train the dogs. I then throw a handful of Rice Chex on the floor and they scramble to eat them. I then head upstairs, turn on G's light to make the first attempts of getting him up;

I take my shower and get dressed. I then head down and reawake Monica who goes back to bed for the forty extra minutes. I take a small stuffed Giraffe (Named Toppers) and tap it on each of her cheeks followed by taking its tail and tickling Monica's nose. I then take the stuffed Ostrich (Named Stretch) and hop it up to Monica's head.

He taps her nose twice with his beak and then sits on her head. I then end up with a kiss and head down. Ok, a bit corny admittedly, but a loving ritual nonetheless.

I go downstairs around 6:20. Liss is usually right behind me. She drinks the drink on the table with her vitamins I left her. She then signals the dogs who are already wagging their tails as soon as they hear her come down as they know what's coming. Liss takes them through a series of tricks followed by each of them getting one of the rice chex after each trick. At the end of the sixteen, whomever did the best gets the reward of the stack of three.

As Liss is doing this, I am heating up coffee for Monica. I bring it up to her where she is usually in the shower. I give her a few sips in the shower and then place it on the counter. I give her a kiss good bye. I then go into G's room. Still asleep I rustle him as I head down. I say good bye to Liss and head into my truck.

On the way to work, I listen to some inspirational audio cd program. I head to Starbuck, get a "Grande Bold, no room with a stopper." Add my sweet and low and head to the office. I enter the building and greet the completely silent and peaceful building and go through each office, looking at what work is being worked on by my teammates to get a sense of where each is. After walking the entire building, I head up to my office and am usually there by 6:45–7:00. A simple walk around the building with coffee in hand gives me a great sense on what is going on in the Firm as a whole, allows me to see who is working on what and in this peaceful, serene, quiet time, it focuses me on the day ahead, before the days frantic pace begins. I go to iTunes and play some loud music as I take the first sips of coffee. I begin to check and respond to emails and begin dictating things for Kristy and develop plans for all the others, begin various management agenda, and all of the other tasks of running a Law Firm. Kristy arrives at 8:30. At 9 the others trickle in. The day then unfolds consisting of all the work for clients, meeting with Kristy once she settles in and various points throughout the day, meetings with fellow team members, as well as contact and communication with all of the others as needed. I do find it important to speak and see each team member daily when possible. As I later head home, I resume listening to motivational or educational audios. I never leave the office until I have completed everything on that day's agenda. I note also that leaving the office does not mean the business day is done. Once home I will field client calls, emails, plan for the next day and interact with my fellow team members.

I come home, eat dinner with the family and then watch some TV. I head up around 8–9 and read for a half hour to an hour. Monica and I connect at night and talk about the day and life in general. In bed by 9:30–10 with a positive podcast or more Howard Stern (Yes, I understand the dichotomy here, but I have been listening to Howard for decades. He provides a sense of diversion for me as well as reinforcing a long-standing ritual.)

So there you have it. A glimpse into my current, daily rituals. I am currently reading a book by that name, *Daily Rituals*. The book contains hundreds of one or two-page summaries of some of the greatest individuals, past and present. Every single one of them had many things that they would do each day that when looked at from outsiders may seem ridiculous, crazy, eccentric, odd or unbelievable. The take away however is that none of them cared what the outside world thought, or would think, as it was what they did and/or needed to create unbelievable results. While I do not pretend to be on the same planet as these individuals, I too live by certain traits, rituals, oddities and many things that the outside world, including you, may think is odd or OCD.

Regardless of your impressions, it is me. These are habits that I can unconditionally say have allowed me to create much discipline and success in my life and that of my family, clients and friends. It is my hope to not only break the mold of traditional lawyers, but to create an individualized mold of my own. While we must listen to those that we trust, and read and listen to advice from those much better than us, in the end, we are unique and must always remain so. To put our stamp on this world, let's strive to leave a crater that will always be associated with us. It is also my hope to make a difference in the world, so I will be forever equated with making positive differences in people's lives that go on to infinity.

That's a day taken from my personal journal from January 31, 2014. So let's look at three years later, in 2017. Over the last year, many things contributed positively to my life. I am still up throughout the night reading and responding to client emails. I now get out of bed to feed and take the dogs out at two in the morning, as they are on their own new schedule. I am back in bed at a quarter after two. I now get back up at six o'clock to head down and take three gulps of a sugar-free Red Bull (just enough to change me from half asleep to a peak state to work out).

I head down into the gym, and with a positive podcast playing, I hit the weights and then cardio. I note that as I write this in the summer, Monica (a teacher) sleeps in as she does not have work. She does her whole routine later in the day. We do exercise together each Saturday and Sunday. Doing this first thing allows me to energize my day by focusing me on the day ahead and making sure that health is a priority of my day and my life.

I began each of the last 365 days by completing a daily exercise in Joel Osteen's 365-day daily planner. This purifies and enriched my day and focused me on something positive. I also did the same thing in leadership expert John Maxwell's daily planner. This focuses me in on something I could add to my team at LaMonaca Law and to my clients, family, and friends while improving personally in this regard.

After I work out with weights, the last part of my daily workout finds me on the exercise bike with my iPad. I answer emails from clients and watch or read several daily video blogs and daily videos by other experts. Darren Hardy's daily video is short, sweet, and empowering. These further focus me on the day ahead.

After exercising, I head upstairs, mix a green drink, take vitamins, and eat a power bar, which energizes me with proper nutrition. I then bring Monica a cup of coffee, shower, get dressed, kiss and hug Monica, wake up Liss and G, and head off to work. Stop by Starbucks, get my "Grande bold, no room," and head to work while listening to an uplifting audio book. I get to work before most people are even waking up, and I plan my day. By the time most of the world arrives at their jobs at nine o'clock, I'm four hours into my day.

While my current morning and office routines remain the same, they now include two additional buildings to survey as I have purchased these in the last few years as LaMonaca Law expanded to one of the largest family law firms on the Main Line. This was not a random occurrence; it was the result of years of planning, a great team, focus, habits, rituals, and a compelling vision. It is through these habits and positive rituals and through working with Monica and other key people to have the same, common vision.

This quiet morning routine allows me to visualize my day and see in my mind what I want to achieve. It is quiet and peaceful—no distractions. Getting to bed early assures I get enough sleep. This extra time in the morning allows me to exercise, journal, and read empowering books and articles. By responding to my clients' questions and concerns well before most offices open, I dispel their fears, answer their questions, and allow them to be at peace instead of having to wait to have their questions answered.

This routine has worked very well for me, my family, fellow team members, and clients, and it keeps me on track. What works for me, however, will not necessarily work for you. Some like exercising at night. What you read and enjoy will be different from what I enjoy. The secret is to not blindly replicate what others do but create positive routines, habits, and rituals that will inspire you to achieve your goals and create a compelling future for you and your family. If your life is lacking in one or more areas, perhaps add something new to your daily routine that will help you break through your limiting beliefs. In doing so, you will find yourself enjoying life in ways that you could not have believed.

What positive habits, rituals, and routines can you add moving forward to catapult you further toward achieving your goals? What negative habits, rituals, and routines will you eliminate that have held you back and negatively affected your life?

13. Follow Your Passion

Passionate people are more successful than are those who are less passionate period. If three people present a topic of interest with identical facts, the one who does so with passion will overshadow all the others every time. We tend to believe people who convey passion in what they say and do. I have the pleasure of meeting many passionate people at the office and elsewhere. I try to surround myself with those who exude passion. I teach my leadership team that it is not about the message conveyed at team meetings but instead about how that message is conveyed. That is the critical difference in being an engaging leader or speaker. In the courtroom, an impassioned delivery allows me to convey my client's message to the court. If you don't appear to believe what you are saying to the court, how can you expect the judge to truly understand and agree with your argument?

We all define passion differently. Does it involve the volume that one projects when conveying a message? Is it in the mannerisms people utilize as they deliver a message? Is it in their conviction? Body language? Passion evokes a subjective feeling in the recipients. How we each define this will be based on how we see the world through our filters. How we were raised, what we observed, our education, life experiences, culture, social networks, and the meanings we attach to things contribute to how we see someone. It will also be the guiding force to the passion we convey to others and how.

I have made the study of influential people a life mission. By reading thousands of books, listening to hundreds of audio seminars and audio books, and by attending dozens of live seminars, I have had the privilege of being taught by the best minds. What each has is a unique flair on conveying a message. I have compared some of the greatest minds and the most influential people and have found that many of their core messages are similar. What made early biblical leaders and leaders from centuries ago successful are often the same traits of modern authorities or are found in their speeches. The difference typically is in the unique delivery styles of the speakers and how they convey their messages.

Motivational legends Brian Tracy and Anthony Robbins have different speaking styles. I've been listening to their messages for decades and enjoy both for different reasons. They share a very common bond—their passion to make others successful and their devotion to effecting positive change in others. If you go according to pace and tone, Brian Tracy is slow, rhythmic, and methodical whereas Tony is a menagerie of styles ranging from yelling to whispering. In my mind, their passion is on par. Zig Ziglar and Jim Rohn as well have separate, iconic delivery styles that are legendary. Watch these speakers on YouTube and see for yourself the differences in their deliveries. Which style do you prefer?

I have seen this firsthand at LaMonaca Law. My meetings with clients take on a life of their own with my volume ranges, body language, gestures, and pace changing based on the client and his or her situation and what I am trying to convey. Inherent throughout, however, is my passion to invoke instant change. I change my tone throughout the meeting incorporating many ranges from low and empathetic to loud and screaming at times based on the circumstances and the outcome I'm trying to achieve. The Brutally Honest system is designed to do exactly that. Historically, lawyers are known to have a rather rhythmic, monotone delivery that evokes confidence by way of a comforting voice. My system is the furthest thing from this. My sessions are tailor fit to the unique dynamics of my clients' situations and needs and are especially designed to alleviate their fears and change their emotional states.

To evoke instantaneous results requires a radically different approach. The sum of these skills makes up my passion that comes out during my meetings. All these changes are genuine and based on empathy, compassion, and my devotion to positively affecting every person I am privileged to meet.

One of the unique attributes of our practice at LaMonaca Law is our team approach. The firm includes teams that comprise supervising attorneys, other attorneys, paralegals, legal assistants, and specialized departments, including a forensic support team and an appellate unit. Based on clients' preferences, they may meet with any one of the attorneys in the firm. Often, clients ask to meet with me first. After we meet, we determine that the client will be handled by another team based on that client's needs, preferences, or requests.

When I meet with clients, I do so in my unique style. Clients meet with me initially in a highly emotional, high-energy meeting that often allows them to leave that meeting with radical changes in their emotional states, which prepares them for the short, intermediate, and long-term things necessary to allow them to achieve their unique family law and personal goals. This system, Brutally Honest, is the subject of books by the same name; it's unique—nothing you will find in other law firms. While the system is utilized by the rest of the LaMonaca Law team members, no one's delivery is quite the same as mine. That's a good thing.

At times, after first meeting with me and then later meeting other attorneys whose passion is the same as mine but perhaps at different volume levels and with different body language, clients may think that our quality is different, but that's not true. Our firm's passionate team members all have unique styles, and that makes us the diverse firm we are. By utilizing our team approach, clients are exposed to a plethora of diverse talent, personalities, and combinations of those that allows them to benefit from the combined efforts of our firm.

Passion to me is more than just delivery and volume; it's synonymous with dedication and determination. I base my ability to maintain my habits and routines over extended periods on my passion to learn, grow, and develop to the point I can apply this information to myself, family, team members, friends, and clients.

As I go from book to book, author to author, speaker to speaker, I grow and learn, increase my knowledge, and fuel my passion. As I speak with my clients, family, and friends throughout the day, regardless of the subject, I learn more and fuel my passion. Thankfully, passion is a work in progress that we can change throughout our lives. As I become engaged with a new author or speaker, I add these positive traits to my personality toolbox to be utilized later to assist me in conveying my message.

I read a book a client had recommended to me. Somewhat the reverse of how I usually do things, I listened to the audio book first, which the author himself had recorded. His style was over the top, loud, energetic, and passionate. I bought his book, and I have listened to dozens of his podcasts and read his other books. His passion and energy motivated me to want to listen to him. His unique style resonated with me; it elevated him above thousands of others whose styles were similar. I in turn have referred him to others and have incorporated his teachings and style into my repertoire.

How do you define passion now? Has it changed since reading this chapter? Maybe? Maybe not? I ask you to consider not being a one-size-fits-all person. Having the ability to change your mannerisms to meet your desired outcome will take you far in this diverse world. With modern forms of media, our ability to convey messages takes on another dimension as it challenges us to be able to convey our messages much faster with symbols, shortcuts, emojis, computers, smartphones, and many other communication devices. Our society has exchanged long lunch meetings with a few keystrokes delivered from afar. Society today rewards and requires instantaneous information. Those in each generation further define what passion means to them. This eclectic and ever-changing world is challenging but also exciting.

Beginning today, instead of simply going from day to day doing the same things, make a conscious effort to adjust your volume, tone, pitch, rate, timbre, and body language and see what happens. I'm convinced that when you do, your life will improve in ways you could never have imagined. Your employer or employees will see a difference, your family will notice, and your life will be radically improved. I'm not suggesting you show up at work in a clown outfit doing somersaults unless of course you're a clown. What I am saying is remember Einstein's famous definition of insanity—doing the same thing repeatedly and expecting different results. If you are happy with your life and do not want to make any changes, keep doing the same things you always do. If, however, you want to make impactful changes in your life, give some of these techniques a shot.

What areas of your life could you improve by adding passion to them?

14. Adapt and Change

As I write this chapter, we are in a whole new world than we were last year or years before. We live in a global world in which information travels far quicker than we can keep up with. Let's take a quick journey back in time.

Ten years ago, there was a thing called the US postal service that delivered things called letters. If I wanted to let my relatives know about things in my life or see photos of the children, I would take out a piece of paper, take a writing instrument called a pen, compose my thoughts, and write them down. I would then go to the drug store and pay for photos I'd dropped off days before. I would open the package and marvel at twenty-four photos most of which were great but some of which were blurry. I would take a copy of a photo (as I paid extra to get two copies of each), place it in the envelope, seal it, pull out my black alphabetical book in which I had addresses for my contacts, write the recipient's address on an envelope—a primitive containment device to enclose documents and letters—with the same pen, lick something called a stamp, and stick it to the envelope. I'd drop the envelope into a blue receptacle called a mailbox, which were located every block or two.

I would then wait a few days or weeks to get a response. I would hear a ring on an instrument called a telephone in my house. What a cool piece of technology that was. It had a hand device where one part would be in front of your mouth and the other by your ear. It was connected to its base by a cord that would more often than not be tangled and worn. The base had buttons of numbers or a dial you turned. Are you millennials jealous yet? I would pick it up and have what they call a conversation. I would actually talk with the person on the other end. We had face time too. We'd decide to actually meet someplace and talk in person. Believe it or not, you can actually still do these things.

Fast-forward to 2019. Things are a little different and are changing by the second. Same scenario as above—I want to send some photos of the children to my relatives. I simply open up the photo app on my phone, Facebook, Instagram, Snapchat, or any of the other countless apps, click on the photos I want to send, and hit a button. Within sixty seconds (that's my time; most kids can do this in under four seconds), I just did what used to take me days to accomplish. My relative sees the information and within seconds and can respond to my photo. They can "like" it and share it with others. If I want, I can hit another button and see them in a live picture and speak to them "Jetson" style by video.

Information and technology are moving at warp speed. In the time it took me to write this sentence, developers from around the world have launched new apps, programs, and technology that are changing the world. Our ability to adapt to this continually changing environment will make the difference in how our lives evolve. At the core of this lie decisions we all must make to adapt or not to this technological tide. While technology clearly can change our lives for the better, it can be overwhelming. What apps do we download? When should I update the hundreds of programs I have on my computer? Should I buy the latest and greatest smartphone? In the course of reviewing these decisions, you may be confronted with several opinions that can conflict with each other—one pundit favors change and another says keep what you have. Google "What is the best football team?" While we all know the answer is the Philadelphia Eagles, you'll be flooded with different opinions. Who's right?

I had dinner with some close friends this past week, and we discussed the latest and greatest changes in technology. It was interesting how different we were. As I write this, Facebook still remains one of the favorite programs to exchange information with friends. That said, it really depends on your generation. Generational differences dictate many of the trends we have and the direction the world is going. At the table were all successful people in their own right. Two of us were Generation Xers and the others were baby boomers. One of my friends (a baby boomer) had never used Facebook and refuses to do so. I along with the other two spent the next few minutes explaining to him the benefits of Facebook—the ability to send photos and instantaneously get up to speed with countless old friends, current friends, and long-lost schoolmates, but he steadfastly defended his lack of interest. He is seemingly happy, extremely successful, and very bright, so who's right?

During our conversation, I and the other two offered what our children were using. This generation, the millennials, and Generation Z (teenagers) look at Facebook as a dinosaur; they primarily use Instagram, text and Snapchat. The trend is going more and more with instantaneous relay of information; many disappear after a short period, and that prompts even quicker replies. Monica and I joke with our children about when she and I started dating at age fourteen. We spoke on the phone for hours and frequently met face to face. Today, that concept is foreign. This instant-gratification generation prefers text messaging over email and Snapchat over Facebook; they're at the cutting edge of technology. Again, who's right? The answer is not so much as who is right as it is having healthy respect for everyone's opinions and to embrace these differences, not fight them.

As I mentioned before, the staff at LaMonaca range in age from over seventy to under twenty—all the generations I mentioned earlier. I embrace the beauty of having input from all these highly diverse team members. I sent around a survey asking everyone what we could do to improve. The answers I got were outstanding and illustrative of the diversity in the firm. Traditional law firms and most businesses for that matter are top-down hierarchies in which unless you are of a certain age and have been with the company for a number of years, you are not expected to have input. Instead, you are expected to simply do your job as directed by those who have been there a while. This old-school mentality has caused many businesses to fail as the old guard sticks to what they know and refuses to change.

Contrary to that mentality, I live in the realm of constant improvement. I read voraciously on a myriad of topics including the future. Ray Kurzweil and Peter Diamandis, who are at the cutting edge of what the future will bring, created Singularity University. They focus on gathering the smartest people to study and opine what the future will bring. Kurzweil created a concept called Singularity—a future period during which the pace of technological change will be so rapid and its impact so deep that human life will be irrevocably transformed and computers will be equal to the human brain.

What life will be like as the years go by will slowly reveal itself. What I know for sure, however, is that much as the world evolved from writing letters on Facebook, Instagram, and Snapchat, it will continue to evolve and more quickly. We can stay fixed in time or embrace the inevitable changes coming our way. I respect your choices in this matter, but I plan to remain vigilant in my unquenchable desire to know what the future brings, to stay on the cutting edge of technology, to read and listen to individuals who are a lot smarter than I am to get their opinions, and to continue adapting and changing.

Generation Now is the collective knowledge, information, and beliefs of all generations; it's an unbelievable amount of data, information, beliefs, and life experiences that when embraced is powerful and gives a crystal-ball peek into the future.

What adjustments do you need to make to change the long-term effects of your goals? What changes can you make right now that will set you on a new path? Will you remain set in your ways, or will you embrace change and what the future holds?

15. Consider Failure as Your Friend

"Failure is your friend? Did he really say that? Did I read that right? After reading all these uplifting and energized words, is he now telling me to forget all of it, to discard my achievements, and instead fail? Has he lost it?"

It may well be that I've lost it, but trust me when I tell you I mean what I'm saying.

The universal theme behind most great self-help books on success is that many of the authors have suffered and failed but have overcome all that and wrote about their ultimate successes. It's impossible to be successful in everything we do. While it's okay to have a healthy fear of everything we do, we cannot let that fear paralyze us. We all fail many, many times. I wrote something that appears in our book *The Brutally Honest Life Management Journal* that sums this theme up nicely:

> "It is through our failures that success seeds are planted. It is through the recognition and learning from our failures that those seeds are fertilized and it is through the willingness to take corrective, future actions that abundant trees reign free." Gregory P. LaMonaca

Life is full of trials and errors and then more errors, more corrections, more learning, self-correction, course correction, and then more trials ... If we had been born with predestination, where everything was mapped out for us, we would know in advance everything that lay ahead of us and we'd be free of fear of the unknown.

Almost all my new divorce clients fear the unknown. Many had been married for years, and some for as many as fifty years. They developed certain habits, customs, and rituals with their spouses, children, and life in general, and the predictability of their circumstances was comforting. All of a sudden—or not as sudden as I typically find—their lives are turned upside down as they are looking to start new lives during the divorce process and then post-divorce. That can be extremely scary and fearful. Doctors, lawyers, entertainers, sports professionals, CEOs and other successful people who in other areas of their lives are in total control and looked to by others for answers all of a sudden feel out of control, scared, uncertain, and not sure what will happen next.

At the core of the Brutally Honest system at LaMonaca Law is our desire to immediately identify what fears and concerns our clients have. By identifying these early and often, we can from the outset help them address their fears and start developing a plan for them to begin down their new road. We let them know that even if they believe no one else is on their side, our entire team is.

One of the top emotions new clients have is a sense of failure. Most people consider marriage as a permanent contract—to death do us part. But that belief has eroded. Many millennials think that marriages can end as quickly as they started, but nonetheless, the majority of people consider divorce a failure.

I have decades of experience in dealing with a myriad of personalities, and I am able to give them hope and help them envision compelling futures for themselves and their families through the fog in front of them, and I can guide them each step of the way. Putting aside for a moment spiritual views of divorce as there are as many views as there are beliefs, I help my clients see the difference between failing in the act of marriage and failing in life. To this end, I allow them to see that notwithstanding their personal culpability and accountability for their actions, divorce comprises many factors beyond their control.

As I mentioned, I have them journal about their relationships from the start to the present day; that has a cathartic effect on them, and it helps me to best guide them through the divorce while systematically giving them tools to move forward and speed the healing process, the learning process, and create a compelling future. By our breaking down what they perceive as failures into their parts, clients are able to first rebuild and then build an even greater future for their families.

Given the unique emotional nature of divorce cases, I become very close with my clients as they share with me the most sacred and intimate parts of their lives. That takes place only after they develop a deep level of trust with me. As a result, I am in touch with the vast majority of my former clients. Almost all report that while they of course did not anticipate getting divorced, now that they have, their lives are much better than when they were simply subsisting in poor marriages. Whether the cause of the poor marriage was abuse, addiction, or simply two good people who couldn't remain married to each other, they begin to see the failure of the marriage as an opportunity to learn, grow, develop, and instill in their families many new traits, including resilience, persistence, courage, and countless others that while once vibrant in their marriages had become dormant in their marriages. Many say that their only regret was waiting too long to move forward with divorce and remaining in a loveless marriage.

Life is in essence a series of failures and successes. It is often only after we fail that we can elevate ourselves to our next level of success. Keep in mind that what makes up one's failure could be another's success; failure is subjective and relative. Not a day goes by that I do not consider something I did a failure, but every day also brings many successes. Because of the relativity of our definition, we often become successful in our minds only by comparing our successes to our failures.

Assume you're doing a chest workout at the gym and decide to bench press. For months, you've been getting stronger and stronger by lifting progressively more and more weight. But you get stuck at the 325-pound mark not being able to get even one rep. Week after week, you attempt that amount, but despite your best efforts, you cannot lift that weight. One day, however, after visualizing your past techniques that resulted in failure, firing yourself up, learning from your mistakes, and developing additional strength and commitment—with an overwhelming desire to improve, you're ready for your next attempt. Your partner is there to support you, you crank up some loud Metallica, sit on the bench, pound your fist, get into a trance, lay back, grip the bar, and lift it—three times. You jump up and high-five your spotter as euphoria overwhelms you.

Your learning from your failures allowed you to obtain success, which you'll carry forward as you evolve through this wonderful thing called life. At any given time, you are the sum of your failures and successes. The meaning you give these milestones will determine how you feel about yourself, how you act, what your outlook is, and where life will take you. By embracing and studying each of the things you call failures and learning from them, you create valuable lessons and are willing to test your boundaries again. You will find that life will afford you an abundance of excitement, opportunity, and fulfillment.

I have created a process called the Teeter-Totter effect. Go to the LaMonaca Law YouTube page (www.youtube.com/watch?v=Mg46DHUN6LU) and see the video I posted about this concept. It's a simple visual I use with clients, family, and friends to show that at any given time, where there is a positive, there is a negative. This is represented by each side of the teeter-totter. When you see a negative, you can shift your focus to a positive. When clients first come to see me, many find it difficult to see anything other than the negative. By using this process, I initially have them commit to at least acknowledging the possibility that a positive side exists, and in time, that becomes a probability. My goal of course is to ultimately have them see that these new, positive things are reality. They learn how to spend a majority of their time focusing on the high end of the teeter-totter.

What in your life did you label as a failure? What did you learn from it? Was it really as bad as you thought at the time? Do you focus more on the high end or the low end of the teeter-totter? What can you do to change this? List ways in which your life is better off with your having gone through it. What lessons did you learn as a result?

16. Lead a Purpose-Driven and Fulfilling Life

Life is an ever-evolving series of challenges and obstacles that allow us to determine what we're made of. While we can somewhat predict what life will give us, we cannot with certainty predict or plan what will actually happen. What does it mean to live a life of purpose? What is our purpose? What do we need? What drives us to achieve our goals? Why am I here? What is my purpose? Despite your religious views, these questions are valid, and answering them will make a difference in your life.

Have you ever felt really upset, down, genuinely unfilled? When you were experiencing these feelings, did you wonder how you possibly felt that way despite many things that were going well for you? Why is this? This chapter will examine why you feel this way, and that will reduce your stress and increase your satisfaction in life.

We all go through times when we feel down or upset and don't know why. Our lives as a whole seem great—good careers, solid finances, and loving families. Why then would we feel upset? That would seem crazy to most, but what people think about us is a chapter in itself.

It's like a pie. You can be satisfied with four slices but not the fifth and sixth. Among Tony Robbins's *6 Human Needs* are "contribution" and "growth," and they're worth learning about. It's helpful to identify this as something real. You can consciously focus on only one thing at a time. Consciously, you focus on your finances and consider them just fine, but your subconscious looks at all the slices of your pie, and the result is that you still feel unfulfilled, upset, and depressed about a slice that's not in your conscious mind then.

The benefit of keeping personal journals is that you can do exactly what I am doing this morning. By analyzing my life in writing, I get to slow down and consciously assess my life the same way my unconscious mind does. While I can never assess as many things as it does, I can analyze and break down my various feelings into different slices. Having done so, I conclude that in my life, my primary needs are to contribute to others and grow personally. Sharing this book allows me to fulfill those two critical needs. Everyone is different as to what of the six slices or needs he or she prioritizes. It is helpful therefore for each of us to understand these six needs and consciously address each. For me, it's by creating Brutally Honest books, online videos, blogs and social-media posts and contributing to the world in this unique way.

Whatever emotion you're after, whatever vehicle you pursue—building a business, getting married, raising a family, being financially well off, being debt free, traveling the world—whatever you think your nirvana is, there are six basic, universal needs that make us tick and drive all human behavior. Combined, they are the force behind the crazy things (other) people do and the great things we do. We all have the same six needs, but how we value those needs and in what order determines the direction of our lives.

Tony has written extensively about the six human needs. If you have not had the pleasure of attending one of his seminars, I strongly recommend doing so. Monica, our children, and I have attended four of his seminars, some lasting four days and others lasting eight days. I have read all his books several times and listened to his audio seminars too many times to remember. One of my habits is listening to certain audio seminars every year at the same times to reinforce the lessons I had first learned from them decades ago. In many of these seminars or products, Tony takes the individual through his six human needs analysis in their own lives. This needs analysis gives you an understanding of each and what your primary ones are that will assist you in becoming fulfilled in life.

Let's look at these six needs; think about your life and how you would rank each. You'll gain a much better understanding of why you do what you do and why others do what they do. You will see why two different people can be fulfilled by totally different things.

The following is taken from a LinkedIn post from Tony Robbins, which was later transcribed in an article written for *Entrepreneur* magazine from December 4, 2014:

Need 1: Certainty/Comfort

The first human need is the need for Certainty. It's our need to feel in control and to know what's coming next so we can feel secure. It's the need for basic comfort, the need to avoid pain and stress, and also to create pleasure. Our need for certainty is a survival mechanism. It affects how much risk we're willing to take in life—in our jobs, in our investments, and in our relationships. The higher the need for certainty, the less risk you'll be willing to take or emotionally bear. By the way, this is where your real "risk tolerance" comes from.

Need 2: Uncertainty/Variety

Let me ask you a question: Do you like surprises? If you answered "yes," you're kidding yourself! You like the surprises you want. The ones you don't want, you call problems! But you still need them to put some muscle in your life. You can't grow muscle—or character—unless you have something to push back against.

Need 3: Significance

We all need to feel important, special, unique, or needed. So how do some of us get significance? You can get it by earning billions of dollars, or collecting academic degrees—distinguishing yourself with a master's or a PhD. You can build a giant Twitter following. Or you can go on The Bachelor or become the next Real Housewife of Orange County. Some do it by putting tattoos and piercings all over themselves and in places we don't want to know about. You can get significance by having more or bigger problems than anybody else. "You think your husband's a dirt bag, take mine for a day!" Of course, you can also get it by being more spiritual (or pretending to be).

Spending a lot of money can make you feel significant, and so can spending very little. We all know people who constantly brag about their bargains, or who feel special because they heat their homes with cow manure and sunlight. Some very wealthy people gain significance by hiding their wealth. Like the late Sam Walton, the founder of Wal-Mart and for a time the richest man in America, who drove around Bentonville, Arkansas, in his old pickup, demonstrating he didn't need a Bentley—but of course, he did have his own private fleet of jets standing by.

Need 4: Love & Connection

The fourth basic need is Love and Connection. Love is the oxygen of life; it's what we all want and need most. When we love completely we feel alive, but when we lose love, the pain is so great that most people settle on connection, the crumbs of love. You can get that sense of connection or love through intimacy, or friendship, or prayer, or walking in nature. If nothing else works, you can get a dog.

These first four needs are what I call the needs of the personality. We all find ways to meet these—whether by working harder, coming up with a big problem, or creating stories to rationalize them. The last two are the needs of the spirit. These are more rare—not everyone meets these. When these needs are met, we truly feel fulfilled.

Need 5: Growth

If you're not growing, you're dying. If a relationship is not growing, if a business is not growing, if you're not growing, it doesn't matter how much money you have in the bank, how many friends you have, how many people love you—you're not going to experience real fulfillment. And the reason we grow, I believe, is so we have something of value to give.

Need 6: Contribution

Corny as it may sound, the secret to living is giving. Life's not about me; it's about we. Think about it, what's the first thing you do when you get good or exciting news? You call somebody you love and share it. Sharing enhances everything you experience.

Life is really about creating meaning. And meaning does not come from what you get, it comes from what you give. Ultimately it's not what you get that will make you happy long term, but rather who you become and what you contribute will.

Now think about how money can fulfill the six human needs. Can money give us certainty? You bet. Variety? Check. Obviously it can make us feel important or significant. But what about connection and love? In the immortal words of the Beatles, money can't buy you love. But it can buy you that dog! And it can, unfortunately, give you a false sense of connection because it attracts relationships, although not always the most fulfilling kind. How about growth? Money can fuel growth in business and in learning. And the more money you have, the more you can contribute financially.

But here's what I truly believe: if you value Significance above all else, money will always leave you empty unless it comes from a contribution you've made. And if you're looking for significance from money, it's a high price to pay. You're looking for big numbers but it's unlikely you'll find big fulfillment.

The ultimate significance in life comes not from something external, but from something internal. It comes from a sense of esteem for ourselves, which is not something we can ever get from someone else. People can tell you you're beautiful, smart, intelligent, the best, or they can tell you that you are the most horrible human being on earth—but what matters is what you think about yourself. Whether or not you believe that deep inside you are continuing to grow and push yourself, to do and give more than was comfortable or you even thought possible. The wealthiest person on earth is one who appreciates. (Anthony Robbins 2014)

Of these six human needs, which two are most important for you? In my family law practice, I ask my clients many questions to elicit their answers to this question. By reviewing their journals, I get great insight as to what ultimately was lacking in their marriages and in their lives. Clients will often be confused about why their marriages dissolved when a review of their journals instantly gives me the answer. Can you imagine what a relationship would be like in which one spouse is fueled primarily by certainty and the other by uncertainty? What if she values love and connection most while he has those at the bottom of his list?

In life, you will not always be matched with a partner who shares your values. What is critically important, however, is to know what needs your partner has and collectively work to meet each other's needs. Failure to do this will result in unfulfilled needs, a loveless marriage, and a lack of connection. By understanding, reviewing, and prioritizing these needs in writing, you will be able to live a purpose-driven, fulfilled life.

By analyzing your needs and comparing them to those of your partner, family, friends, or anyone else, you gain a better sense of what you and they need to be fulfilled, and you start finding ways to honor and fulfill each other's needs. Those who focus on only their needs often find themselves confused about why others fade away from them and avoid them, and they lose valuable relationships.

At LaMonaca Law, I speak with countless clients who are beyond confused as to why their marriages dissolved. They openly and honestly tell me that they have not changed, that they are loving and caring and gave 100 percent to their marriages. After I ask some focused questions, what confuses them becomes obvious to me. In their journals, I ask them to write about their marriages and describe their spouses and what they like or do not like. A client may say that after she and her husband worked hard to become financially secure, they spent quality time together just cuddled up on the couch and watching television. Contrarily, her journal tells of her husband spending six days a week playing softball in multiple leagues followed by hanging out at bars after each game. If she places love and connection as her numbers 1 and 2 and her husband places significance and uncertainty as his numbers 1 and 2, it becomes evident to me why they drifted apart.

This does not mean that to be successful in marriage, both spouses need to have identical needs. On the contrary; it's through the healthy differences we have that love can shine. Exchanging and sharing each other's passions are at the core of healthy relationships that grow. The key word above is *sharing*. By understanding what fulfills your partner, by taking time to learn what makes each other tick and what each other's goals are, you will develop collective objectives that will help your relationship thrive, not just survive.

Balance is the key in healthy relationships. It is as important to have collective goals as it is to have individual passions. Having your own identity is an important part of a healthy relationship. By balancing your private objectives with the relationship objectives, by evaluating them often, and communicating to make sure you both understand each other, you will have a fulfilled life.

Ask yourself, *do I have a defined purpose? Have I reviewed Tony's six human needs and determined what my primary ones are having ranked them? Have I shared them with my significant other, family, and friends? Do I have shared as well as individual passions? I will commit to the following …*

17. Teach Your Children Financial Literacy

The greatest gift you can give your children is that of financial literacy. We started giving our children age-appropriate lessons about money at age three, and not just saving but actual investing. In addition to the typical toys, clothes, and gifts at Christmas and birthdays, we bought them shares of dividend-producing stocks and mutual funds. In addition to their cartoons and movies, we worked into all car trips educational audio programs that taught them how to be better individuals and how and why to invest.

They've actually interacted with our accountant and financial planners since age five. They read about their stocks in small snippets they can understand. They came to look at investment properties with us and the realtor and learned the process. With minimal investments started at this early age and consistently applied each year combined with the magic of time and compound interest, they will have many more options than if they had not invested or waited till after college or age thirty or forty to start saving and investing. Fast forward to 2019. They are both in college and will soon graduate debt free. This did not just happen. It goes back to those early days of teaching them the same lessons that you are reading now, based upon a long term plan put into effect by Monica and I, followed by perhaps the most important part, taking ongoing, consistent action toward the attainment of these goals.

More important than the money, our children learned financial literacy at an early age. When they were young, we read about and implemented age-appropriate ways to help them understand the value of money. Many people have touted this approach, so I'm not sure who gets the original credit, but we followed many of them and had fun doing so. The way it goes is that you create three jars with the first labeled "savings," the second "investing," and the third "charity." We told them what each one meant, and when they received their allowances or other money, they put a third in each jar.. Most pundits of this approach advocate using thirds, but you certainly can change the allocation to fit your beliefs. The point is to have them do it, not you. By doing so, they feel empowered as they see their money working. We would then have them contribute a dollar from their charity to the collection plate at Mass each week. This instilled a great satisfaction and pride in them as they were able to help others. Each year around Christmas, when we would make charitable donations to Children's Hospital of Philadelphia and A.I. DuPont Children's Hospital, they too would give up 1 of their Christmas gifts and use the money to contribute.

One of my favorite pages in any book I have read as it pertains to finances is a chart appearing on page 48 of *The Automatic Millionaire* by David Bach. This is one of the most powerful lessons anyone can teach a child and even their parents. It shows the time value of money in three situations.

> **Billy:** Billy starts saving $3,000.00 a year beginning at age 15 and does this for only five years till age 19 and stops investing. With compound interest doing nothing else (assuming a 10% annual return which of course could be higher or lower but it makes the point) at age 65 he has $1,615,363.40.

> **Susan:** Susan waits four more years from Billy and begins investing at age 19 and invests $3,000.00 a year for 8 years and then stops investing. At age 65 she has $1,552,739.35. Despite investing for three more years than Billy, because of her delay she ultimately has less.

> **Kim:** Kim waits twelve more years from Billy, and eight more years from Susan and begins investing at age 27. Kim then starts investing $3,000.00 a year each and every year up to and including age 65. At age 65 she has $1,324,777.67.

This chart demonstrates in one picture the time value of money and the effect of waiting to invest. I recommend everyone read this fantastic book cover to cover. If parents see this early enough and begin investing many years before Billy did, perhaps as soon as they are born, by setting up accounts, encouraging relatives to give monetary gifts instead or in addition to presents, what do you think their financial state would be at age sixty-five?

Parents can make a game out of teaching their children these lessons by using any one of the countless, free, online financial calculators that demonstrate this. You can change the start date, the amount invested, the rate of return, and the end date. Their eyes light up, and parents themselves are often mesmerized and wonder why they hadn't done this themselves earlier.

Okay, as I have mentioned a few times, many of you feel you have too many student loans and other debts, are unemployed, or any other number of life's real events. I hope you don't spend your valuable time focusing on the problem but instead on identifying the problem and spending most of your time crafting the solution.

Try this fun and interactive lesson. Tell your children to grab five toys they haven't used in a year. Go online to find out their costs when new. Add them up and put this dollar amount in the financial calculator to show what those dollars would become by the time they retire. This is but one way of making financial literacy fun to learn. You'll enjoy giving your children pearls of wisdom and will be solidifying their futures.

I know that if I walk throughout my house right now, I'll spot hundreds of thousands of potential dollars sitting in every room. How many items did you buy that at the time you felt you had to have? How many of those items now sit in a closet? Imagine going back in time, thinking about the purchases, and not buying them but rather investing the money. Go ahead—put the dollar amount in the calculator. Would you rather have that money compounded or that item in your closet? We don't have a magic wand to do that with our past expenditures; we can put this idea to work with future purchases.

Think about a coat you bought ten years ago for $100.00. I clicked an online money/time calculator and put in that $100.00 as present value, 10 percent yearly interest, and ten years. It came out to $259.37. That dusty coat simply taking up space actually cost you $259.37. Even if the market dropped 25 percent, your investment would still be worth $194.51. This is an example of one item in closet. How many similar items do you currently have sitting around the house, in your garage, or in an attic? Think about selling them in a garage sale or on eBay and converting them into assets for you and your family. This exercise can be a fun family project.

When the children were young, we gave them shares (albeit few) of stock on their birthdays and at Christmas. As we drove around, we had fun looking out the car window to see the different stocks they owned—McDonald's, Exxon Mobil, and many others.

Everything in life is relative. What we learn is in direct proportion to what we observe, listen to, and believe. Here in America, we find it hard to believe that there are still aborigines who wear loincloths, live in primitive houses, hunt food with homemade spears, and wear war paint. As we watch this on TV, we are spellbound and amazed that this could still be going on. The aborigines, however, would look at our lives the same way. This is not limited to aborigines or those in remote lands. As you read this, throughout the US, there are millions of different views and perspectives on what's best, how to live, and how to become happy.

We've taught our children from early on that we are the sum of what we have learned in life. Our family has been learning, growing, and developing together as we have shared all of these lessons together. Remember the analysis of Tony Robbins's six human needs in the last chapter. I discussed the importance of understanding your partner's needs, and this also applies to families. It is important to have individual needs, relationship needs, and family needs. In our family, we have made the process of learning fun. As a result, understanding finances and investing is as normal to them as eating grubs is to aborigines.

Those who follow the lessons in this book will find themselves and their families very well prepared to be in the best financial position they can be in this ever-changing world. Life expectancies are increasing, and that underscores the need to start early in securing a long, healthy, and prosperous retirement. Regardless of your age, you can always begin today to save and invest and teach your children to do so as well.

Many adults in their thirties, forties, fifties, and sixties have no investments and inadequate retirement savings. I have started a movement in this regard by spreading this message. Adults of any age can begin to stop the bleeding with certain focused planning, and I believe they have an obligation to create this knowledge base in their children so they can run with this knowledge and pass it on. If high school children have no financial literacy, savings, or investments, I consider that their parents' fault. While that may be a controversial statement, I stand behind it. Teach your children to ask themselves, *Can I simply get the small fries as opposed to supersizing? Do I need that shirt that says "Look at me—I made it?" or can I wear the one I own that says, "Love me—I'm a work in progress"?* I hope you look at every purchase as money burned compared to what it could be years later if you invested it. Sacrificing today by utilizing delayed gratification will allow you to live an abundant life in later years. As Dave Ramsey says, "If you will live like no one else, later you can live like no one else."

The only things certain in life are death and taxes. No one knows what tomorrow will bring—economic crises, terror attacks, and health issues could be among them. We cannot predict the future, but we can minimize its adverse effects. As demonstrated above, it does not take being a member of a rich family; instead, it takes only a willingness to learn as much as you can about financial literacy (and you can find so much online for free) and share that knowledge with your children. I listen to dozens of free podcasts on every topic as well as financial literacy. Using these sources to learn and reinforce this knowledge throughout life will ensure lifelong financial literacy.

Here is another novel approach—books! Books seem to be a dying breed these days. Gone are the days when most people relied on libraries and bookstores, but that's not the case with my family. We love heading to a bookstore and wandering the aisles looking for any information we need. We have also been going twice a year to a used book sale in town. Some of the greatest books you would ever want sell for twenty-five cents or a bag of books for five dollars.

Stop making excuses. Take personal accountability for your and your children's lives. If you truly want knowledge, it's out there for free in most instances. You simply need to take action!

Ask yourself, *What investments can I provide my children this year for their birthdays, holidays, and so on? What knowledge can I share with them that they can learn from and have fun doing? Where can I take them on a family road trip to make learning fun? What audio podcast can I download right now to listen to individually, and as a family? What fun can we have organizing a yard sale or selling things online?* Regardless of where life finds you financially, you can make your life better with a little planning.

18. Develop a Team

Going through life alone is lonely and boring. It is almost impossible to become successful, content, or happy based solely on ourselves. We are the sum of our interaction and involvement with others. Throughout life, we are voluntarily and involuntarily members of many teams.

From birth, you were placed involuntarily on your first team, your family. We don't choose our families, but we can choose what we do on that particular team. My family is the center of the bull's-eye. Throughout my life, in good times and bad, my mother, father, and two brothers were an integral part of my life. We have supported each other to this day with unconditional love. I was fortunate to have been raised in a family where Mom stayed home, Dad worked, and we all ate dinner together at the table each night. While we were never rich in monetary terms, we were wealthy in love and the way we all supported each other growing up right through today.

When I met Monica at age fourteen, we formed the early makings of our team. As one of eleven children, she too was the product of traditional family values. With that many people living in a small home, teamwork was essential. It was also crucial that the leadership structure be adhered to. What Mom and Dad said had to be the rule if they wanted to avoid anarchy in the household. Monica was likewise fortunate to have been raised in such an environment. Unfortunately, her mother and father— two of the greatest—were taken from this earth too early, but the sense of teamwork they instilled in their children allowed them to flourish and continue to support each other in a loving spirit today.

When Monica and I married and had Alyssa and Gregory, we formed the next wave of our team that has flourished because of the family values she and I had learned growing up. While the world today is different from what it was when we were growing up, the core principles and values are the same. I am fortunate to have all four of us together in a loving, supportive environment.

As I'm typing these words, I'm waiting for them to arrive at our vacation home in the Pocono Mountains. I came up to work remotely a couple days ago, and they will join me for the Easter weekend. The four of us will enjoy each other's company, no doubt get on each other's nerves, play games, go to the bookstore, and celebrate Gregory's birthday. But this too will pass. Life will evolve. Alyssa attending West Chester University locally, and Gregory is away at college this year. Despite these inevitable and exciting changes and regardless of where we are, we're a family unconditionally and will always support each other through thick or thin as a team. We are far from perfect; we make mistakes, but we always make sure to learn from them. We truly have "unconditional" love.

As the founding member of LaMonaca Law and after having practiced family law for a quarter century, I have seen the range in the continuum from loving, supportive families to severely abusive, dysfunctional families. In my early days working for the team at the public defender's office, we represented indigent clients who could not afford attorneys. Thousands of cases were each riddled with different levels of tragedy and dysfunction. At one point, I ran the juvenile division representing children who had committed every imaginable crime. What I learned to appreciate was that if you look only at the outcome, the crime, you can easily form conclusions about these children, but when you delve further into the lack of a team environment they grew up with and lack of stable families, while the behavior is not to be condoned, you learn to empathize with them and understand their situations.

In many areas, crime at an early age is the norm that children are conditioned to accept. They either adapt or face possibly being killed. Crime is all they know. They idolize their brothers who are in jail. That's very difficult for most others to accept and appreciate without having walked a mile in their shoes. Given that most of these children came from broken homes where there was often not a mother, father, or siblings, they developed other teams to take their places—gangs. They learn the rules and regulations to survive in the group and in their towns. Early in my career, I learned to not judge a book by its cover.

I later rose in the office to work on adult trial teams; I represented indigent adults who likewise had been raised in a variety of environments. The empathy I learned early on allowed me to represent each of them with compassion and with an understanding of not just what they did but why they had done it. There are no excuses for crime, but understanding the backdrop and ingredients that went into making up each client allowed me to zealously represent them and put their cases in perspective for the judge, jury, and society.

My career evolved, and with Monica by my side, I opened LaMonaca Law firm. I am privileged to have represented thousands of clients from diverse backgrounds, families, and life circumstances all of which make up the teams they are on. LaMonaca Law represents clients from all socioeconomic classes. Much like indigent clients are stereotyped, so too are the affluent. It is popular to believe that the rich are fortunate to be able to provide for their children and families in ways the indigent cannot. Money does afford opportunities those without it cannot take advantage of, but it also provides temptations. Some of the most dysfunctional teams and families I have been involved with were affluent, but their children were left alone, or they had the autonomy to throw sanctioned drinking parties, or they had money to buy drugs. Some showed no direction as their parents were traveling the world—rehab after rehab and many other problems. This is certainly not indicative of all the affluent; on the contrary, it is the minority. I mention this simply to dispel the rumors and stereotypes about each class.

I can tell you firsthand that many of the families in my son's and daughter's former high school allowed and sanctioned drinking in their homes by their teenage children and their friends. Their belief is that it is better to allow them to drink safely in their homes and to stay over than it is to drink and drive. While I understand why they think the way they do, I do not condone it and instead take the stance that it is illegal and will not be accepted in my home or elsewhere.

That said, I also understand that as a rite of passage, teens will likely experiment with alcohol and other illegal things. We expressed our beliefs to our children in logical ways that we hope set in. We have also stressed the consequences if they choose to stray—punishment at home of course but also perhaps court records that will follow them the rest of their lives.

Life affords us countless opportunities to join teams other than our families—sports teams at all sorts of levels, scouting, political parties, martial arts clubs, high school and college organizations, on and on. At some point, we join the workforce and enter various teams in our jobs.

LaMonaca Law today has the greatest team—currently, nineteen members—we have ever had, but we did not start off as one of the largest family law firms on the Main Line. I have been blessed with a team of individuals who work tirelessly to support each other, empathize with our clients, and live to help others. The team is based on loyalty, and the length of services averages over ten years. Our whole team shares our culture and core values. As all teams do, we have issues that arise at times, but we have systems to deal with them and quickly move past them in an atmosphere of respect for each other. I am truly blessed to have the privilege of working each day with such an outstanding team.

The best teams share traits and factors that make them successful; no one can get by on his or her own. While we can fumble through life guessing right at times and wrong at others, surrounding ourselves with a team of advisers will give us a significant edge. The key is having the right advisers—the wrong advice from the wrong people can be devastating.

Monica and I have a CPA, lawyers, financial planners, insurance agents, and other professionals who provide us with information. They advise us on matters they specialize in, and that frees us up to do what we do best. We don't always take their advice, but we trust them to give us their best and give us a different perspective at times as to how we can best achieve our goals.

While this chapter has identified many of the teams in my life, it is not all inclusive. I'm on other teams directly or indirectly and affiliated with many others. As new teams are added, others might go by the wayside or become dormant. In my study of successful people, I have learned that they all appreciate their teams.

What teams are you on right now? Whom can you add to your team today to create your own board of advisers? How can you become a better team member?

19. Focus on Your Health

Physical fitness by way of weight lifting, aerobics, martial arts, and so on has been a constant that has always been with me through life's many trials and tribulations. Those who have read *The Brutally Honest Life Management Journal* know of my long battle with a very rare health condition that for a while made me one of the oldest if not the oldest patient at Children's Hospital of Philadelphia. I had a tumor on my spine that paralyzed me for a long time and required surgeries plural, but I not only survived; I thrived. I had other benign tumors throughout my body since I was fourteen, and I've suffered disabling injuries, broken bones, and too many symptoms to mention. Through it all, however, I was committed to my health, exercise, and mental focus.

I write this chapter well over three and a half decades after I started to lift weights. My father was a lieutenant colonel in the US Army. Each year, he would go away for two weeks, often to Fort Dix Army Base in New Jersey. When I was fourteen, he took me to spend a few days with him. That was an incredible experience; I spent that time with my dad, whom I idolize. He taught me leadership, and I saw the great respect he received as we walked around base. There, he bought me a set of sand-filled, eight-pound weights. I sat in the car outside the PX and opened the box they came in and read the exercise plan. I stepped out of the car, lifted my first set of weights, and became hooked for life.

After seeing how I had taken to the weights, Dad bought me an affiliate membership at Holiday Spa in the Granite Run Mall in Delaware County, Pennsylvania. I became obsessed with fitness there. After Holiday Spa, I moved on to the YMCA and local gyms and had a good stint at Olympus Gym in Havertown, Pennsylvania, where extremely loud, heavy-metal music blasted out of speakers. I heard weights being dropped and smelled the sweat equated with hard-core lifting.

(Interesting note: As I'm proofreading this chapter, my Bose headphones have Motley Crüe cranked up to the highest volume playing "Home Sweet Home." Coincidence? I think not. lol.)

The place was not a sweet-smelling gym like today where you spray down the benches after each set and people have headphones on and are in their own worlds. There, everyone knew everyone, helped everyone, yelled, screamed, and had one hell of a good time. Working out was my priority every day. It was there that I had my 1,100-pound leg press with my close friend Chris Mattox (now the Honorable District Judge Mattox) standing on the machine as I stacked ten 45-pound plates on each side filling each side of the bar. I did a 500-pound squat and bench-pressed 110-pound dumbbells. My friends, my brother Steven, and many others all worked out there every day. It was a culture of fun, family, and friends competing, getting fit, and having fun.

Once I began college at West Chester University (WCU), Monica and I would drive together. Between classes, and after, I worked out in the campus gym. After classes, we went to work all night—no socializing, partying, or hanging out. We worked, worked out, worked on our relationship, and stayed focused on our goals. I started an internship at Kmart in the security department my last year at WCU. After graduation, I remained there and was offered the position of head of security. Despite my obligations with classes, work, family, and my relationship with Monica, I always exercised.

At two times during these years, my medical condition caused me to be out on disability. Benign tumors randomly came up at various times of my life and in different parts of my body; they caused me to go from lifting massive amounts of weights to not being able to lift my arm on its own, hip joints fusing, broken bones, torn muscles, and periods when I couldn't walk. Radiation treatments, surgeries, and countless tests. At no time regardless of my disabilities did I ever stop lifting weights and doing cardio. If my left arm could not work, I'd put my right arm to work with a fifty-pound dumbbell, go back on the bench, and bench press with one arm while using every stomach muscle on my left side to keep me from flipping off the bench. When my legs didn't work, I used a cane to get to the pull-up bar and did massive numbers of pull-ups and push-ups as well as upper body work.

When I was in my early twenties, my brother Joe, a pilot, would fly to the Bahamas on occasion. He invited me to go with him and some friends. It was an amazing trip that still ranks as one of the most special times Joe and I spent together. Our hotel, though not a Four Seasons, was nice. Unfortunately, it had no gym. So we scoured the maids' room, found some broomsticks, took towels from our room, took the cooler we had, filled it with ice, and made a makeshift barbell with ice for weights. Push-ups with our feet on the bed. Dips using chairs. Resistance on other exercises provided by Joe or me pushing in the opposite direction of the broomstick as the other pushed the other way. With a little creativity, we improvised and had one hell of a workout. No excuses—just great fun!

From my first day in a karate dojo as a white belt through the many years of training through black belt and beyond, I broke several more bones, dislocated joints and fingers, and suffered countless other injuries. As I wrote in my prior book, I was told that if I took a kick on one of the tumors in my ribs, I could bleed to death. Mom was staunchly against my continuing training, but Dad supported me as I simply wore rib protectors. That didn't stop me from breaking my ribs, however. When I did, I would acknowledge the pain, figure out how it limited me, figure out what I could still do, and do that.

One night, I skipped my evening law school classes, met up with my close friend and workout partner Jim McCoy in his basement (which we named the dungeon in honor of its concrete walls and hard-core equipment; it was a cool place to work out.). As I psyched myself up to do a bench press with hundreds of pounds on the bar with Metallica cranked up in the background, I lifted the weight, and as I gently started down, I heard three loud *knocks* as the weight rapidly collapsed and converged on my chest. Thankfully, Jim was there to spot me and pull it off. If not, I might still be pinned to that bench. I went to the ER and learned I had shattered my collarbone. Apparently, a tumor in that area had weakened the bone. Guess where I was the next night as my arm was in a sling? Back in the dungeon using all my other available limbs to work out. Jim went through many physical problems as well, but he always found a way to be there. We supported each other through illnesses and injuries and had one hell of a fun time doing so. More than any muscle, my mental conditioning, creativity, the support of Jim and other workout partners, and an unwavering commitment has kept me going.

I sit here decades later in my home office typing these words and focus on my body, which has countless aches, pains, and disabling issues. Notwithstanding, I get up weekday mornings around five o'clock (some days it may be the afternoon or seven in the morning on weekends), head down to the kitchen, take three gulps of Red Bull, and head down to my basement, stretch out, acknowledge what limitations I may have that day, and work my ass off with weights followed by cardio. No excuses. All this before most of America gets out of bed. This routine allows me to clear my head and focus on the rest of the day. Vitamins and good food fill in the rest of the picture.

The point of this chapter is not to impress you but to impress upon you that barring some extraordinary circumstances, everyone can and should exercise and live healthy lifestyles. My close friend Jim Grim, coauthor of our first book, recently passed away after three courageous battles with cancer. As he was in the hospital getting stem cell transplants and after massive doses of chemo, he made a makeshift gym in a storage room in the hospital, and that helped him physically and mentally. He amazed hospital staff as they saw him do things that they didn't consider possible. They were impossible for them but not for Jim. He was a warrior who lived by the warrior's code up till the end. So yes, there will be times when you may not be able to do anything, but barring such extraordinary circumstances, figure out what you can do, set goals, and begin pursuing them today!

My commitment to my health grounds me and keeps me physically and mentally fit. Exercising is as much the norm for me as are breathing and eating. Since we met at age fourteen, Monica has joined me in this passion to exercise. Alyssa and Gregory achieved third-degree black belts in their teens, and they continue to train and teach the martial arts carrying on a tradition I had. It is a family value at the core of our beliefs.

I write this on a Saturday morning. Unlike during the week when my workouts start my day at five o'clock, on weekends, I come down to my office, write in my journal, or like today, write a chapter in this book. As I conclude this chapter, it's nine in the morning. Monica just knocked on the door and had her coffee, and together, we are headed to the basement gym to—yes, you guessed it—do weights and cardio.

What exercise program can you start today? Do you need to gain weight? Lose weight? What achievable goals can you set? Get off the couch and take a walk. Instead of focusing on what you cannot do, implement a plan for what you can do today!

20. Focus

As we discussed earlier, the law of attraction states that you get what you focus on. Did you ever wonder why one night you are paralyzed by intense fear and worry but you wake up feeling elated and on top of the world? What changed? The same facts were there when you went to bed as when you arose. The difference is focus. At any given time, you are consciously thinking about any number of things. Try it now. Think of a red door. What did you see in your head? Chances are not a green door. Life works the same way. If you think about your retirement funds being cut in half, your job possibly being eliminated, and health problems, you'll no doubt feel miserable. If, however, you ask yourself, *What am I grateful for?* You will be more inclined to focus on that. Your focus can increase in many ways, including by getting proper sleep and nutrition, writing down your goals, keeping a journal, maintaining daily, positive habits and rituals, listening to and reading empowering information, and eliminating as many negative things in your life as you can.

At LaMonaca Law, we focus exclusively on family law, one of the most complex and emotional areas of law. It takes an exceptional personality type to work in this area. As I mentioned in the introduction, when we hire team members, I look for special individuals whether for an attorney, paralegal, or legal assistant position. While the schools people attended and the grades they achieved are important, even more important is what they have inside. Are they resilient? Thick skinned? Can they solve immediate, life-threatening problems? Can they be creative? Do they possess outstanding communication skills? Are they empathetic and compassionate? Can they go over and above 24-7 to assist clients in this very emotional area of the law? Can they maintain a high level of focus while helping clients get through their unique roadblocks? Can they think outside the box to help our clients create compelling futures for themselves and their families?

Because of the above, our interview process is highly unusual, but it increases our chances of recruiting the best of the best—team members who are most suited to working in this area of the law. I recently told one of our clients that the value I provide to them is 20 percent my knowledge of the law and 80 percent my ability to provide decades of experience and focus all my resources on their unique goals. All attorneys must read statutes, file legal papers, and attend court hearings and do so effectively. It is in the unique way they go about those tasks that separates the good, the very good, and the outstanding attorneys.

Just this past week, I met with three new female clients. Each one was well educated, healthy, and well off financially, and they all had husbands who had cheated on them, belittled them, and threatened them to some degree physically, emotionally, or financially and had also threatened to take their children. Each of these clients was emotionally drained with self-esteem at all-time lows. I told them each not to worry about what anyone else thought about their situations; what mattered was what they thought; that would ultimately make the difference.

I am proud to offer an approach to initial consultations that differs from those of my colleagues. Mine can run a few hours because I want to make sure the potential client leaves with a new sense of hope, a subsiding of their fears, determination, and a plan to create a compelling future. By working with them, I strive to have them see things through a different lens and filter. Quite simply, you get out of life what you focus on.

A client I met yesterday shared with me that she had been depressed for many years; that had been debilitating and at times made work difficult if not impossible for her. She brought this up several times to defend her reasons for having done or not having done something. This type of depression is pervasive and can genuinely take over someone's life; it doesn't magically disappear simply by wishing or hoping it away. That said, many things can be done to minimize the effects of these feelings or plant seeds that begin to overcome them.

At that first meeting, after identifying the fears my clients have, I begin changing their focus. I offer them real-life examples of similar cases I have assisted clients with; I have them visualize what their lives will be after they eliminate their fears; I give them tools they can use right away. By my simply being caring, compassionate, and empathetic, they leave our meetings with a new sense of purpose, hope, clarity, and most important, a real plan to help them overcome their fears, create a compelling future for themselves and their families, and know that it is not only possible but probable. They understand it will take a lot of work and effort and a laser focus on what will be. I believe strongly in the benefits of having other professionals such as counselors, psychologists, MDs, or others with expertise help with the unique problems presented.

Like the individual mentioned in the beginning of this chapter who went to bed paralyzed by intense fear and worry but woke up the next day feeling elated and on top of the world, the three women changed their focus and saw, felt, and believed what was probable. They immediately changed the direction of their lives toward the positive. I assisted them in distinguishing between fact and fiction. What were their real legal problems, and what were simply perceived as such? What fears were real, and which ones were not?

Many dismiss this positive-thinking stuff as a crazy belief system used by self-help gurus. It's interesting how I have evolved in my defense of these contentions over the years. I often spent countless hours debating the naysayers on this, but I discovered this type of battle cannot be won, and I found the critical difference and secret of life. This secret changed my approach, my feelings, and my life. The secret is to live and lead by example.

There is no better proof than success. In the end, regardless of your beliefs, the outcome of your beliefs will be the proof of them. Instead of debating the matter, I started showing them the outcome of these types of beliefs. As this book has revealed, this type of thinking and belief system is not simply legal theory or personal case studies. It is the very real way I have lived and continue to live my life and the things I teach my family, friends, and clients. These lifestyle changes and beliefs have worked for me and those in my life. What better proof is there than that? So there are no more debates. A debate implies that there are two potential perspectives. My living and leading by example and showing it has worked eliminates this needless back and forth. I respect those who disagree with my views or beliefs; if they have better ways I can use, I'm all ears because I always want to improve myself.

New clients give me the opportunity to help them believe they too can change their beliefs and lives. It all starts with that first shift in their focus. By giving them real, relatable examples of similar clients (with no breach of anything confidential) who have been in their position and have changed their futures by changing their focus, they begin to take the first critical steps to creating their compelling futures. The incredible thing is that once they achieve this transformation, they get hooked on sharing this positive information and lifestyle with others.

This past month, we ended a two-day custody relocation trial in which we convinced the court to allow our client, an amazing, caring, and loving mother, to relocate to another state for her and her children's benefit. The thank-you letter we received was heartwarming and validated why we do what we do. It was also rewarding to read that she was going to make sure she continued to pay it forward. As family law attorneys dealing with some of the most emotional and complex cases, we can become disheartened at times, so getting a letter about how caring, generous, and compassionate we were was rewarding and a great tribute to our entire team at LaMonaca Law.

What can you do right now to change what you focus on? What can you do to eliminate whatever is distracting you? What can you do to add a better sense of focus and clarity in your life? Your life changes the moment you decide to change, so do it today—now. Write down three things you'll do today to positively change your focus, and do them!

21. Associate with Like-Minded, Positive People

One way to increase your focus is to associate with like-minded, positive individuals. I have a core group of family and friends I associate with because they empower me and add value to my life. They allow me to ask questions and gain their perspectives on topics or ideas I'm thinking about. I trust them unconditionally; I know they want the best for me at all times and will give me their true feelings, not what they think I want to hear. I share my thoughts with them in an environment of trust. Just the act of spending time with them empowers and motivates me. It brings out my creativity and lets me break through barriers. Seek out those who can provide you with many resources, add fun and enjoyment to your life, and allow yourself to eclipse your self-imposed barriers.

It's easy to associate with those we see all the time such as family, friends, and work associates. More often than not, associating with them adds value to our lives. With family, we have no choice; we were born into our families, and with work associates, we again had some discretion when it came to where we chose to work, but for the most part, we see our coworkers daily and can develop bonds with them. And our friends originate from different sources—our neighborhoods, schools, sports teams, and other groups.

By using the lessons in this book, you will find useful tools to make any of your relationships stronger. Throughout your life, you will have many opportunities to create bonds with different people and groups, but remember the adage—you'll become the sum of the top five to ten members of your peer group. Whom you spend the most time with will have a dramatic impact on your life, who you will become, your potential, and what you will achieve. I use the analogy of a bull's-eye. In the center will be your closest and most trusted individual. Each successive ring going out is one step removed from the center with the importance slowly lessening as you move out. Your family will have the earliest impact on you at some of the most critical ages where your personality, beliefs, and attitudes are created. I was lucky enough to be born into a middle-class, loving, loyal, and supportive family. It was traditional in a sense for that era—my father worked while my mother stayed home to take care of us. In my life, my family makes up the closest rings of the bull's-eye.

When I was growing up, I was friends with the kids in my neighborhood. I participated in team sports and later individual activities such as martial arts. Over the years, our initial peer groups tend to dissolve as they spread out all over the country, so they leave the center of our bull's-eyes and are replaced by others when we go to college and get married. Life evolves; so too do those in the rings of our bull's-eyes.

Today, I am blessed to have several of my grade school friends in my closer rings as we have stayed in touch and live close to each other. Since first grade, Tommy and Kevin have been there for me as I have tried to be there for them. Kevin is one of my closest friends whom I interact with many times each week. He is an adviser to me in business and in life. My children know him as Uncle Kevin. Tommy is one of the most consistent, principle-oriented individuals I know. My earliest friend, who lived across the street from me in grade school through high school, lives in New York with his wonderful family, and he's a very successful businessman. It's been decades since I've seen him, but he's in my thoughts. Mike J is both another grade school friend and talented Patent attorney.

College can create many close friendships. Monica and I attended West Chester University, but we never had the time to party or socialize with others that much because we worked after classes, but I did make friends with those I worked with at Kmart after college, and I'm friends with many of them on Facebook. One of them is Chris Mattox; I'm his beautiful daughter's godfather as he is to my Alyssa. He worked at LaMonaca Law for a long time before becoming Judge Mattox.

During that time, I met one of my closest friends, Jim McCoy, my workout partner I mentioned in the chapter on health. We shared a passion for fun, games, and lifting weights. Chris, Jim, and I would stay up all night playing video games at my house to the complaints of my parents. Today, Gregory does the same thing as he interacts and plays with all his friends online.

After college, I went to law school and met friends I am privileged to still share close relationships with. Tim Rayne is a local award-winning personal injury attorney, Kevin Fasic is an outstanding attorney in a

Delaware firm, Phillip Aronow is a tenacious and talented prosecutor in the New Jersey Attorney General's office, and Bill Francos is a brilliant patent attorney. Through law school, after school, and over the last twenty-five years, our families have remained close and get together periodically. We refer work to each other based on our specialties and are loyal to each other.

Since LaMonaca Law started in the spare bedroom in Monica's and my first home, I have met thousands of clients, and some have become close friends with whom I have shared many great times, including parties, special occasions, and trips. Among them was Jim Grim, whom I represented in a custody case. We became close and shared family values, passions, and interests; we created Brutally Honest together. He was truly a brother from another mother. He and I spoke several times a week. His advice, guidance, and love were integral parts of my life. He and his wife, Cyndii, opened the award-winning Ultimate Image Salon and Spa in Exton, Pennsylvania, and we were often sounding boards for each other's business. Kevin would never be caught listening to positive audios or reading motivational books, but Jim and I lived in that world and exchanged all of these types of products. Given that Jim originally despised anything self-help but did a complete 180 on the matter, I figure there remains hope for Kevin. Lol.

This book spanned many years and went through many revisions. It pains me to know that as I proofread this section in May 2018, Jim is no longer with us after his three battles with cancer. He was taken from us far too young earlier this year. His death reinforces the lessons in this book—we should cherish everyone in our lives and proactively reach out to them.

I have had the privilege of working with some of the most talented, loyal, and compassionate individuals at LaMonaca Law. Many of our team members have been with me for over a decade, including Kristy, Larry, Chris M (now of Counsel), Carol, Lauren, Joe L (also of Counsel) and of course Monica. Others such as Alicia, Chris C, Brady, Andrew, Jenn, Christina, Patricia, Patrick, Alyssa, Theresa and recently Gregory along with all the other team members form my family away from home.

What I enjoy most is the loyalty, friendship, camaraderie, and trust we share.

Notice I waited till the end to define the inner rings of my bull's-eye. Clearly, the friends mentioned above and team members at LaMonaca Law are in this range. As we get closer to the center, there of course are my mother, father, and brothers Steven and Joey. They were my earliest and most loyal and trusted members in my life. They have added to my life in ways that a lifetime could never pay back. I love them unconditionally, the same way they love me. Other close family includes Uncle Nick, who has always treated me and my family very well. I would be remiss if I didn't mention my other relatives who are no longer with us, including my grandparents, Aunt Josie, Cousin Harry, and many others who positively impacted and helped shape who I am.

While the inner circle of my bull's-eye is reserved for the closest person in my life, it is somewhat shared with Alyssa and Gregory. They are two loving, caring, respectful, passionate, and amazing adults. Coincidentally, I write this on Father's Day. I know they will move out eventually, but for the time being, Monica and I are blessed to have them home with us.

I reserved the innermost position in my bull's-eye and in my life for Monica. I could never adequately express how much I love her. Since age fourteen, we have been together through the ups and downs and every other conceivable time. She redefines what unconditional love is. She lives for me and the children above anything else. Whatever the highest degree of loyalty is, she eclipses it. She is one of a kind in all the best ways. She grounds me and keeps me real. I mention often to others that our relationship is not only a true success story but also a true, old-fashioned love story. Is that bragging? You bet. You can't argue with success. By success, I mean creating and maintaining unconditional love.

So that's who makes up the progressive rings of my bull's-eye. I apologize for those I may have not mentioned—too many people to name. With each layer getting closer and closer, your trust, confidence, and willingness to freely share will increase. With time, the layers may shift—some will leave your rings while others enter them. There's a direct correlation between who you are and who makes up these layers.

Perhaps you need to replace certain individuals in your rings with others who have become more important to you. I tell my divorce clients who find themselves eliminating spouses from their inner rings to replace them with others who will support them.

Napoleon Hill came up with the idea of mastermind groups many years ago. His idea was to create a group of people who will share empowering ideas with, lend advice to, and support each other. These can be physical groups, but they could also be virtual groups that take advantage of todays' technology—online, at seminars, through books, podcasts, and many other media. I have met often in smaller groups or in mastermind groups I organized with Jim Grim, Kevin S, Steve Du, Steve R, Bill A, Glenn M, Tim R, Steve D, Linda M, my brothers Steve and Joe, the Honorable W.M., Robert O, and many others. These individuals and groups have acted as my life's board of director whose members advise me in many areas. Many thanks to all of them, to all those mentioned within, and to those countless authors who wrote more books than I could list.

Whom in your life can you meet with who share similar goals, visions, and values? What opportunities can you take advantage of online or elsewhere to create virtual Mastermind groups? What seminars can you attend? What groups can you join to have fun, help each other, learn, and grow?

22. Old School vs. New School

We are living in a time that allows us to live lives of abundance. A life full of opportunity is often a keystroke away. Drones delivering packages to us within hours, autonomous cars, longer lives, and many other innovations are here or coming soon. Depending on when you are reading this, it may already be here. Gone are the days when we turned to physical encyclopedias or dictionaries. All you millennials or younger, those were actual books we'd pull off a bookshelf, page through alphabetically, and actually read definitions. lol. Today, I use my Amazon Alexa and simply ask it for anything I need, and it immediately responds with that information—instant gratification. I own over twenty of them, and they are in most rooms of my house and in each office at work. The question that remains, however, is whether this technology helps or hinders us.

I once asked one of my attorneys if he was plugged into Alexa, and he said he feared the technology was being monitored. He was fearful of who may be monitoring him. A little overboard or paranoid? Not really. Stories like this are everywhere. Life would be easy if we could sit in a closet, stare at a wall, and feel fulfilled—no pressure, but also no pleasure. As you venture out of that closet, out into the world, you will notice that it is full of opportunities, thousands of them confronting you every second. No doubt it can seem overwhelming and daunting at times. If you took a second to think how much was going on every second, you would be brought to an abrupt, fearful stop. Let's try. Put your hand on your chest as if you were making the Pledge of Allegiance. Feel your heart beat. That's the outcome of the billions of things occurring in you this minute without your consciously thinking or knowing it. We rely on our internal systems to work flawlessly.

The world works much the same way. We consciously observe or think about some things, but other things are occurring worldwide— good and bad—without our knowing them. As I write this, this past year has seen terrorists strike many places throughout the world and here in the United States. Terrorists have taken the lives of fathers, mothers, sisters, brothers, friends, brave soldiers, and courageous first responders.

The tragedy and sorrow these acts bring are unimaginable. How has this affected you? Has it made you afraid to leave your house? Have you changed vacation plans, or have they simply stopped you in your tracks as you watched the aftermath on television? Regardless, my point here is that if you focus on these types of things, you'll be saddened and contemplate a life of avoidance.

Now, picture yourself and your family in Tahiti and in a vacation cabana in the middle of blue waters in the most peaceful and serene environment imaginable. Picture yourself sitting on the deck or floating in the azure-blue waters. What are you thinking now? I would suspect a feeling much different from the examples above.

Regardless of how you feel about the world in general, what I think we can agree on is that it's full of options for us all. When my parents and grandparents were growing up, they were limited in their options. Or were they? This dichotomy is what I refer to as old-school versus new-school thinking. Depending on your age, the definition of this will differ. To me, old school refers to the way things were when I was growing up and earlier, while new school is today and the technology we have. Which is better?

One might routinely say that we are better off today with all the benefits technology offers us. I'm often asked this. I had dinner with my good friend Tommy last week. As mentioned in the last chapter, he and Kevin are two of my closest and oldest friends. They along with another close friend, John, were my grade school friends. Life happens; John and I have not had many opportunities to get together lately. We all met in first grade and have stayed in touch all these years, but as all the others have gone in many directions, Tommy, Kevin, and I live close to each other, debate each other, agree, disagree, and all other things good friends do. We support each other.

At dinner, Tommy and I caught up and reminisced about the old days—when we were growing up. We lived in a blue-collar neighborhood in row houses with parents who married for life.

In the mornings during the school year, John, who lived across the street, and I walked to school—no bus—and passed his mother, Mrs. C, a long-standing crossing guard. She would always have words of advice and caution alike, and she gave us welcoming smiles each morning. She would watch over all of us to make sure we stayed on track. John and I would walk to Tommy's, and the three of us would walk to school. At times, we would ride our bikes home for lunch and back. Can you imagine that happening today?

After school, we went home, did homework, played outside, and had dinner with our families. Divorce was rare in our circles then. We all played sports together and hung out. Yes, I mean out—we went outside to interact with each other. Did we mess up? Did we get in trouble? Did we do things that make us shake our heads now? Absolutely.

As Tommy and I reminisced over dinner that night, we agreed that that was one of the greatest times in our lives and neither of us would have traded it for anything. We didn't come from financially wealthy families, but we had been blessed with a wealth of love, support, and values that remain with us today. We did not have the internet at our disposal, and cable television was just beginning. We learned the old-fashioned way— through school and the school of life exchanging ideas in person.

Fast-forward to 2018. We are blessed to be living during a time when technology has flourished and will continue to do so in ways we can't imagine. Peter Diamandis described the way the majority of individuals think—in a linear fashion. They think that two follows one, three follows two, and so on in a nice line. However, Diamandis thinks the world is progressing in an exponential fashion—it goes from 1 to 2, 4, 8, 16, 32, 64, and beyond. With this rapid evolution, life as we know it is evolving at warp speed in ways the average individual cannot contemplate.

I am fortunate to have completed Peter's Xponential Advantage program, an intense, interactive seminar that taught this way of thinking about the future. This and reading his and his colleagues' books on the topic have allowed me to use this knowledge to radically transform my and my family's lives. I have been able to further use this information at LaMonaca Law with all my fellow team members and clients.

Through the internet, robotics, artificial intelligence, virtual and augmented reality, nanotechnology, and many other areas, life as we know it will afford us an abundance of opportunity. An average life span of a hundred and beyond may soon be the norm. They speak of a world in which sensors implanted in our brains will let us connect with the cloud and instantly provide information to our brains. Where we now use the internet to access Google to read about anything we need, with the future technology above, it will be instantly transferred right to our brains simply by thinking of it. Linear thinkers cannot contemplate such extreme steps, but exponential thinkers see this as not an if but a when. Just another of life's many splendors.

Life as we know it will transform us in unimaginable ways. Think back ten, twenty, thirty years or more. Would you have ever thought it was possible to do the things we do today? The future is likewise filled with unimaginable things that will nonetheless happen.

So which is better, old school or new school? For each of us, this answer will vary. I like the 20 percent old-school and 80 percent new-school scenario. The divorce rate has skyrocketed. Divorces today, while still emotionally difficult, do not carry the same stigma as they did in the past. The norm is now two parents pursuing careers while raising their children but dropping them off at a bus to get to school rather than letting them walk there. Many old-school ways are gone.

Football, stickball, and baseball games on the streets have been replaced by computer games with virtual team members playing via the internet with online friends in virtual worlds. Shopping for clothes will become a matter of letting your body be scanned at your home to ensure a perfect fit and receiving the results delivered by drones within hours.

I believe we must preserve and honor our past by extracting all the wonderful things it has taught us and combine that with present technology to create a life of abundance for our family and friends. It's extremely difficult to stop doing things we have done for years or even decades and be convinced that a new way is better. We can all think of many people who refuse to use the internet, social media, and online banking. My father was one of these. Then he found out he could participate daily with his friends all over the world to exchange information and some not-so-appropriate jokes. lol.

The takeaway from this chapter is that we are living in a world that is changing at an ever-increasing rate. There is no right answer to what percentage of old school vs. new school you should have, but as I tell my clients, at least be open to what the future will bring and embrace changes that improve your and your family's lives.

Evaluate your life right now. What percentages of your life are old school and new school? Are you happy with that, or should you change it in some way? What could you change that could instantly improve the quality of your and your family's lives? What tasks could you combine to make you more productive? What beliefs, habits, or rituals can you modify or change to improve your life? What could you read or listen to that could open your mind to new possibilities?

23. Keep a Journal

This piece of advice is worth its weight in gold. This idea has been at the cornerstone of my success in life and my ability to conquer obstacles. My personal journal has served as my friend, mentor, counselor, and sounding board, and it will be a legacy for my children and grandchildren. It contains over 1,400 pages describing my successes and failures. It's my way of capturing what happens in my life. During all of life's ups and downs—slides and subsequent rises in the economy, good and bad health, good and bad days—I utilize my journal to capture my thoughts, feelings, and what went right and what went wrong. In either scenario, I learn and grow.

Think about how much is going on in your life—billions of bits of data flow through your mind every day some consciously but most unconsciously. What you consciously think about is at the forefront of your mind. Think about how many things you did today. On a grander scale, you worked, and you spent time with your family. At the microscopic level, look at any vein in your arm. Think about how much activity has gone on there in the last few minutes. Think about the millions of interactions that are going on inside you automatically to sustain life. As I have said many times throughout this book, you get what you focus on. My mentioning your veins brought them to your conscious mind. Life works the same way; you can change your thoughts instantly. All you have to do is understand that this is possible and then do it! You certainly can randomly turn this part of your conscious mind on and off. I suggest, however, that you do so in a formal, planned manner. How do you do this? Your journal is a central part of this.

What you use as your journal is not as important as using one. Some traditionalists like to use physical books they write in. Many contemporary thought leaders still use this method and talk about having bookshelves of their journals going back many years. I keep these types of journals in my home office. While I do not write in physical journals anymore, I appreciate their historical significance. I also enjoy reading the journals of successful people past and present. Unlike a book written for others, a journal is personal and will include details from deep down, where this level of honesty can provoke change. A book is like someone who appears at work each day showered, well dressed, with makeup, jewelry, matching colors, suits, ties, and so on. The person walking into work is the product of all these products and processes meant to give off the image of a polished and well-groomed self. Our journals, however, are the raw versions of ourselves that wake up before we add all the things above. That version is our most real, unfiltered, and true self. That is the version of myself I capture in my journal.

One benefit of my older, written journals was that I could draw pictures and diagrams. Over the years, I have shifted to an online, written, password-protected journal. The benefit of this was that I could include more and save it online. I can go back and insert things. As I write this, my journal is over 1,400 pages long. The format you use is personal and less important than the fact that you actually use it.

After you decide to use a journal and decide on the format, the most important part is to begin. You are not being graded. There are no right or wrong ways to include information. My suggestion is to simply begin. I like things to flow chronologically. As such, I keep adding to it as events happen and typically no less than once a week.

There was a time I would write it in every day. These days, I get up early on the weekends as I did today, a Saturday morning at five thirty. I went for a brisk walk outside, I got my coffee, added some loud music into my headphones, and go back over the last week and capture its highlights and lowlights. Doing this allows me to reflect on all the great things that happened the prior week as well as the not so good things. How often you write in your journal is up to you.

Remember when I had you think about the vein in your arm and bring to your conscious mind the blood flowing within? Journaling performs a similar conscious reflection. As you write what occurred in the past, with each stroke of the pen, pencil, or keyboard, you bring to your conscious mind what's happened in your life. The act of writing or typing these things in and of itself will bring them higher and higher into your conscious mind. As is the case with lessons you learn in a book, you are implanting in your mind real, relevant, and impactful thoughts. Capturing these memories—when, how, and why they occurred—will help you learn a success formula you can use in the future. What went wrong in your life? Why did it go wrong? What did you do about it? These lessons are equally important as they also train you how best to move forward in life.

Writing daily or weekly will bring to light events when they're fresh in your mind. Periodically, however, you can go back in your journal to refresh your conscious mind about events that have shaped your life. Tell me what you did on January 18 this past year. Can you remember? If you are like most of us and do not have a photographic memory, you will not remember. When you have a journal, however, you can access these memories in seconds. As you go back to that date and read what was going on, it will bring back to your conscious mind the good, the bad, and the ugly. This is a powerful way to capture and later reflect on life's many blessings.

My journal is the best motivational speaker on the planet. As life evolves and you face inevitable hurdles, all you need to do is go back in your journal to a time when you confronted something similar, review how you addressed it then, and use that information to get you through your current situation. A number of the most influential and successful people have written biographies. There, right in front of you, is your biography in the making, your personal journal, your road map to success.

My journal is my most prized possession in the world. I give Monica electronic copies of it periodically, but she has never read it. She knows that when I leave this great world someday, my journal—the history of my life—will go to my children, grandchildren, and further on. What a wonderful thing to give children and family. In life and beyond, while money, fame, fortune, notoriety, and countless other things may be nice, in reality, we live for a short time. My journal, however, will be my perpetual legacy.

At LaMonaca Law, journals form the cornerstone of our practice and the Brutally Honest system. When clients hire me, I give them two assignments. The first is to give me the history of when they first met the other side right up to the present. In the end, they give me the story of how they got to where they are and most important, the why. This journal allows me to get up to speed and into their heads as to what got them to this point, what problems exist, what fears they have, what makes them tick, what makes the other side tick, and many other pearls of information that will allow me to help them.

I then tell them homework assignment number two is to keep a password-protected journal each day of what is going on in their lives as their cases evolve. They give this to me periodically so I can get up to speed with them, immediately address their fears, understand their goals, see what has caused problems in the past, things to avoid, things to replicate, and many other useful tools. This also becomes a powerful tool for the client to first use as a catharsis and a way to organize their thoughts to best help me help them. Finally, once their case is over, they now have the foundation for a tool to use the rest of their lives, a guidebook on how best to live the next phases of their lives.

A journal is a free, powerful tool that can radically change your life for the better, give you a way to get things out of your head, allow you to learn from your life and stay on track, and become an outstanding legacy for future generations.

Begin today keeping track of your thoughts and ideas and what is happening in your world. What benefits can you immediately obtain by utilizing a written journal?

24. Get a Coach

Due to the many roles we play in life, all the responsibilities we have, and all the goals we're trying to reach, we can easily drift off course. Someone serving as our coach can motivate and direct us and most important hold us accountable to staying on track.

I've used coaches all my life. When we are left to ourselves, even the most well motivated among us can get off track when life happens. Good coaches learn your motivation, mannerisms, excuses, visions, and compelling reasons to succeed. They recognize and are in touch with your goals, values, impediments, and self-imposed barriers, and they can kick you in the ass when you need it. As is the case with many of the things we discussed, it is imperative to get the right coach. Even well-intentioned individuals with many credentials don't always match up with everybody.

Merriam-Webster defines *coach* this way: "A person who teaches and trains an athlete or performer: A person who teaches and trains the members of a sports team and makes decisions about how the team plays during games: A private teacher who gives someone lessons in a particular subject." I have had the pleasure of having coaches who fit all the roles in that definition. I have been coached by my parents from the time I was born to this day. They were my first teachers. Through their direct lessons, their indirect direction, and by my observations of them, they have shaped me and have taught me what it means to have respect, love, leadership, loyalty, and a strong work ethic. They have taught me about family values and how to act as husband, father, brother, relative, friend, leader, and in many other roles. Today, as they still remain happily (okay, full disclosure—they do have their occasional, old-school, Italian moments) married, they have shown by example what family values are all about.

My brothers, Steven and Joey, have been there for me and with me every step of the way and have coached me in many ways. As brothers do, we have loved, laughed, fought, and got in trouble with each other, but in the end and to this day, we support each other unconditionally.

My extended family, including those who have passed on, have taught, coached, and conditioned me in many ways. Consistent with the themes above, they have taught me what old-school family values are all about, what the true definition of family is, and what loyalty means. Unconditional love means just that; it's not situational but enduring and without conditions.

My closest friends are those I met in grade school as well as a select few I have met over the course of my life. In the blue-collar, suburban neighborhood of Clifton Heights, Pennsylvania, we created some of the most cherished memories, and I learned many lessons early on. We lived in row houses where everybody knew each other and doors were often left unlocked. We played outside every day and hung out every weekend in the surrounding neighborhoods. Contrast that to today where kids spend most of their time hanging out online. We played sports and were coached by some of my first formal team coaches in baseball, basketball, football, track, cross-country, martial arts, and many other sports. I owe many thanks to my coaches and friends for lessons learned.

I would be remiss if I didn't thank the countless authors who have shaped my life dramatically. The thousands of books I have read contributed to who I am. They added to my understanding of the many beliefs the world has to offer. I read voraciously every day. Add to them individuals such as Tony Robbins and many others whose audio books, programs, and podcasts I have listened to and whose live seminars I have attended. All these sources have shaped my beliefs. They allow me to consider—note the word *consider*—ways to conduct myself. Often, I may listen to someone whose beliefs are different from mine because that allows me to consider other beliefs and see things from a different perspective. That may move me closer to their ways of thinking, or it may strengthen my firm, opposite beliefs. Either way, they all serve as my teachers and coaches.

All the thousands of clients I have represented and am representing have taught me lessons that have shaped who I am as an attorney, advocate, and leader. They have allowed me to see the world from different viewpoints. They have exposed me to a vast array of beliefs, methodologies, parenting styles, and countless other ways of seeing things. I have had the pleasure of standing side by side as we have passionately argued for family values, parental rights, constitutional protection, fundamental rights, civil liberties, and as many other pursuits imaginable. In courthouses throughout Pennsylvania, New Jersey, the rest of the United States, and internationally, I have had a front-row seat to shaping their and their families' lives. I have learned empathy and compassion as I passionately stood up for them and their goals.

To all my colleagues who represent the opposite sides of cases, I say that while we may not always agree, and while we vigorously debate, argue, and advocate for opposite positions, I value you for upholding in your unique ways your values, passion, and commitment to the law, the Constitution, and the rights of clients everywhere. Through our interaction, whether we agree or not, I learn and grow from each of you.

To all the dedicated masters and judges who give of themselves daily to ensure that justice is served in their courtrooms, I say that while I may not always agree with your rulings and decisions, I always have the utmost respect for the incredibly tough jobs you have as you strive to do what is right.

I would be remiss if I did not thank Coach Doug Pederson of the Philadelphia Eagles. As I have said throughout this book, I wrote and edited it over several years. This entry is being written on February 4, 2018. Today, the—no, *my*—Philadelphia Eagles have just won Super Bowl 52! I cannot put into words how excited I am. They were touted as underdogs all year, especially when future hall of famer and league MVP (if he wasn't injured) quarterback sensation Carson Wentz was injured and backup Nick Foles came in. Not only did they quell all doubters; Nick Foles also became the Super Bowl MVP.

With seconds to go in the first half, on fourth down, when the entire world readied for a chip-shot field goal, Doug Pederson decided without hesitation to go for it. Even I was yelling, "What are you doing?" As the viral video later showed, Foles walked over, looked at Doug, and asked, "Philly, Philly?" Instantaneously, Doug said, "Yeah, let's do it." Nick went back to the huddle and called the Philly Special, and the rest was Super Bowl history. The craziest play you ever saw resulted in Trey Burton getting the ball on an end around whereby he threw the ball to Nick for a touchdown. I have watched the replay at least a hundred times. Here is a coach who made aggressive calls all season even when doubted because he had the conviction to lead and trust his instincts, players, and the process.

We are exposed to coaches every day who take the form of everyone and everything. Whom we elect to follow or have in our lives is up to us. We will take different turns; what we believe today may be radically different tomorrow. With each day, especially in this ever-changing technological world, we will be exposed to thousands of viewpoints. Perhaps more important than your viewpoint is your willingness to be open to other points of view, allowing yourself to be coached by others, and always learning, growing, and improving.

How could your life improve by utilizing a coach? Whom can you bring onto your personal team? Whom could you coach and mentor to improve their lives? Whom do you share similar passions with that together you can coach each other, share common interests, and have fun doing so?

25. Say Thank You

Ladies and gentlemen, we have reached the last of the "Twenty-Five to Thrive." This book has invited you into my world. As with any book that contains the beliefs of the author, this one contains information you might disagree with. That's okay; that makes America great. Simply being born here or becoming citizens allows people to participate in the constitutional rights all citizens have. We are privileged to be living in the greatest time and place on the planet. We have the freedom to respectfully voice our opinions. I have done my best to live up to that in this book. While you may disagree with me at times, I can tell you, as a great football coach tells his players, that I've left it all on the field.

This book contains my thoughts and suggestions on things you can immediately implement if you choose to do so that can make a difference in your and your family's lives. These chapters are not full of theory; they contain actual things I have used successfully in my life that form my core values. It is not my intention to have you model every one verbatim. To the contrary, I have continually taken bits and pieces from countless sources and matched them to my personality, goals, and values to add another dimension to my life.

I end this book with this theme, as I believe it is one of the most important things we can do in life and is one of my most important core values. One of the first books I wrote (that has not been released yet), *The Average Joe's Guide to Marketing in the New Millennium*, has that title as its first chapter. The importance of saying thank you cannot be overemphasized. Far too many times, we take for granted the countless people in our lives who have helped us get where we are. How many times have you taken time to thank them? How many times have you picked up the phone to let them know how grateful you were for their assistance in your life? This little act is powerful and can work magic on the recipients and yourself. I have my wife, children, parents, brothers, and family to thank first. Next, my friends, team members at LaMonaca Law, all my loyal clients, and all the authors whose works have fueled my passion for life and achievement.

In life, we will achieve many levels of success personally, in business, and with our families. We should take time to recognize the scores of individuals who have assisted us throughout our journeys. None of us goes through life without the help of many people who have contributed in their own ways to make us who we are.

While this may be the end of our journey together, it's only the beginning of the rest of your life. What you make of the next level of your life is up to you. I sincerely hope that I was able to make a positive difference, however slight, in making the next phase of your journey successful. As I pass this torch to you, take pride in knowing that regardless of your past, your future is full of possibilities that can change your legacy.

Thank you for taking the time to complete this book and for being one of the exceptional few (we refer to them as the 3 percent) who truly want to make a difference in their lives, in the world, and take action to do so. Very few read books, and fewer finish them. If you are reading these words, you are among this small and elite group. Let this be the beginning of the rest of your life fueled with motivation, passion, and a never-ending quest for information. I am humbled and grateful that you honored me by letting me share my thoughts with you. If you have found value in this book, please recommend it to family and friends and leave a review on our website, www.LaMonacaLaw.com, Facebook page, www.facebook. com/LaMonacaLaw/, Google, https://goo.gl/UXE8pn,

AVVO.Com, our Brutally Honest Facebook page at www.facebook. com/Brutally-Honest-291452130562/, and other areas where we can be found. Likewise, share your thoughts with me at Greg@LaMonacalaw.com. Last, please visit us at all our other social-media outlets, at, or, depending when you are reading this, any other place where we can be found where you can get updates, information, and free downloads, including my book *The Pennsylvania Divorce, Custody & Financial Survival Guide*. Thank you!

Last exercise: ask yourself, who can I thank and *What will I do today to implement the strategies in this book?*

Notes

Notes

Notes

Notes

Notes

Notes

Notes

Notes

Notes

Notes

Notes

Notes

Notes

Notes

Notes